ECONOMIC ISSUES, PROBLEMS AND PERSPECTIVES

2013 ECONOMIC WELL-BEING OF U.S. HOUSEHOLDS

INSIGHT, ISSUES, DATA

ECONOMIC ISSUES, PROBLEMS AND PERSPECTIVES

Additional books in this series can be found on Nova's website under the Series tab.

Additional e-books in this series can be found on Nova's website under the e-book tab.

ECONOMIC ISSUES, PROBLEMS AND PERSPECTIVES

2013 ECONOMIC WELL-BEING OF U.S. HOUSEHOLDS

INSIGHT, ISSUES, DATA

BARRY SUTTON
EDITOR

nova publishers
New York

For permission to use material from this book please contact us:
Telephone 631-231-7269; Fax 631-231-8175
Web Site: http://www.novapublishers.com

Library of Congress Cataloging-in-Publication Data

ISBN: 978-1-63463-118-1

Published by Nova Science Publishers, Inc. † New York

CONTENTS

PREFACE

Chapter 1 – Many households in the United States have been tested by the Great Recession. Large-scale financial strain at the household level ultimately fed into broader economic challenges for the country, and the completion of the national recovery will ultimately be, in part, a reflection of the well-being of households and consumers. Because households' finances can change at a rapid pace and new opportunities and risks may emerge, such recovery can be complex to monitor.

To better understand the financial state of U.S. households, the Federal Reserve Board conducted a new consumer survey, the results of which are described in this report. The Survey of Household Economics and Decisionmaking (SHED) was conducted by the Board's Division of Consumer and Community Affairs in September 2013 using a nationally representative online survey panel. The purpose of the SHED was to capture a snapshot of the financial and economic well-being of U.S. households and the issues they face, as well as to monitor their recovery from the Great Recession and identify perceived risks to their financial stability. It further collected information on households that was not readily available from other sources or was not available in combination with other variables of interest.

Chapter 2 – This appendix to the Report on the Economic Well-Being of U.S. Households in 2013 prepared by the Consumer and Community Development Research Section of the Federal Reserve Board's Division of Consumer and Community Affairs (DCCA) issued July 2014.

In: 2013 Economic Well-Being
Editor: Barry Sutton
ISBN: 978-1-63463-118-1

Chapter 1

REPORT ON THE ECONOMIC WELL-BEING OF U.S. HOUSEHOLDS IN 2013*

Maximilian D. Schmeiser, David E. Buchholz, Alexandra M. Brown, Matthew B. Gross, Jeff H. Larrimore, Ellen A. Merry, Barbara J. Robles and Logan M. Thomas

EXECUTIVE SUMMARY

Many households in the United States have been tested by the Great Recession. Large-scale financial strain at the household level ultimately fed into broader economic challenges for the country, and the completion of the national recovery will ultimately be, in part, a reflection of the well-being of households and consumers. Because households' finances can change at a rapid pace and new opportunities and risks may emerge, such recovery can be complex to monitor.

To better understand the financial state of U.S. households, the Federal Reserve Board conducted a new consumer survey, the results of which are described in this report. The Survey of Household Economics and Decisionmaking (SHED) was conducted by the Board's Division of Consumer

* This report and survey (issued July 2014) were prepared by the Consumer and Community Development Research Section of the Federal Reserve Board's Division of Consumer and Community Affairs (DCCA).

and Community Affairs in September 2013 using a nationally representative online survey panel. The purpose of the SHED was to capture a snapshot of the financial and economic well-being of U.S. households and the issues they face, as well as to monitor their recovery from the Great Recession and identify perceived risks to their financial stability. It further collected information on households that was not readily available from other sources or was not available in combination with other variables of interest.

Key Findings

This report presents findings from the September 2013 survey. The survey covered a range of topics—including household financial well-being, housing, credit availability, borrowing for education, savings, retirement, and medical expenses—meant to round out the understanding of how households are faring financially.

Overall, the survey found that many households were faring well, but that sizable fractions of the population were at the same time displaying signs of financial stress:

- Over 60 percent of respondents reported that their families are either "doing okay" or "living comfortably" financially; another one-fourth, however, said that they were "just getting by" financially and another 13 percent said they were struggling to do so
- The effects of the recession continued to be felt by many: 34 percent reported that they were somewhat worse off or much worse off financially than they had been five years earlier, 34 percent reported that they were about the same, and 30 percent reported that they were somewhat or much better off
- 42 percent reported that they had delayed a major purchase or expense directly due to the recession, and 18 percent put off what they considered to be a major life decision as a result of the recession
- Just over half of respondents were putting some portion of their income away in savings, although about one-fifth were spending more than they earned
- 61 percent reported that they expected their income to stay the same in the next 12 months, while 21 percent expected it to increase and 16 percent expected it to decline

The survey asked questions about a number of specific aspects of households' financial lives:

Homeowners

Homeowners' outlooks for their local housing markets were generally positive

- A plurality of homeowners expected house prices in their neighborhood to increase over the 12 months following the survey, with 26 percent expecting an increase in values of 5 percent or less and 14 percent expecting an increase in values of greater than 5 percent
- Less than 10 percent of homeowners expected house prices in their neighborhoods to decline over the 12 months following the survey
- 45 percent of homeowners who had owned their home for at least five years reported that the value of their home was lower than in 2008, 20 percent believed the value of their home was the same, and 27 percent believed it was higher than in 2008

Renters

Many renters seemed to express an implied interest in homeownership

- The most common reasons cited by renters for renting rather than owning a home were an inability to afford the necessary down payment (45 percent) and an inability to qualify for a mortgage (29 percent)
- 10 percent of renters reported that they were currently looking to buy a home

Credit experiences and expectations

For some, perceived credit availability remains low

- 31 percent of respondents had applied for some type of credit in the prior 12 months
- One-third of those who applied for credit were turned down or given less credit than they applied for

- 19 percent of respondents put off applying for some type of credit because they thought they would be turned down
- Just over half of respondents were confident in their ability to obtain a mortgage, were they to apply
- Experience with credit appears to vary by race and ethnicity, with non-Hispanic blacks and Hispanics disproportionately likely to report being denied credit, to put off applying for credit, and to express a lack of confidence about successfully applying for a mortgage, though these effects are partially explained by other factors correlated with race/ ethnicity and credit, such as education

Financing of education

The perceived value of borrowing to fund postsecondary education varied widely depending on program completion, type, and major

- 24 percent reported having education debt of some kind, with 16 percent having acquired debt for their own education, 7 percent for their spouse/partner's education, and 6 percent for their child's education
- Among those with debt for education, the average amount of all education debt (both for the respondent's and others' education) was $27,840, with a median of $15,000
- For those with each type of education debt, the average amount of debt for respondents' own education was $25,750; $24,593 for their spouse/ partner's education; and $14,923 for their children's education
- Some households struggle to service this debt, with 18 percent of those with debt for their own education indicating that they were behind on payments for these loans or reporting that they had loans in collections
- Among those with debt for their own education, those who failed to complete the program they borrowed money for were far more likely to report having to cut back on spending to make their student loan payments (54 percent versus 39 percent for those who completed) and to believe that the costs of the education outweighed any financial benefits they received from the education (56 percent versus 38 percent for those who completed)

- Among those with debt for their own education, the respondent's field of study appears to impact whether they believed the lifetime financial benefits of their education outweighed the costs of that education

Savings

Savings are depleted for many households after the recession

- Among those who had savings prior to 2008, 57 percent reported using up some or all of their savings in the Great Recession and its aftermath
- 39 percent of respondents reported having a rainy day fund adequate to cover three months of expenses
- Only 48 percent of respondents said that they would completely cover a hypothetical emergency expense costing $400 without selling something or borrowing money

Retirement

Many households reported that they are not prepared for retirement

- Almost half of respondents had not planned financially for retirement, with 24 percent saying they had given only a little thought to financial planning for their retirement and another 25 percent saying they had done no planning at all
- 31 percent of respondents reported having no retirement savings or pension, including 19 percent of those ages 55 to 64, and 25 percent didn't know how they will pay their expenses in retirement
- Among those ages 55 to 64 who had not yet retired, only 18 percent planned to follow the traditional retirement model of working full time until a set date and then stop working altogether, while 24 percent expected to keep working as long as possible, 18 percent expected to retire and then work a part-time job, and 9 percent expected to retire and then become self-employed
- The Great Recession pushed back the planned date of retirement for two-fifths of those ages 45 and over who had not yet retired

- 15 percent of those who had retired since 2008 reported that they retired earlier than planned due to the recession, while only 4 percent had retired later than expected
- Social Security Old-Age benefits were commonly included as a source of funds for people currently retired (74 percent), followed distantly by defined benefit pension payments from work (44 percent) and savings outside a retirement account (32 percent)

Medical expenses

Paying for medical care was challenging for some households

- 34 percent of respondents reported going without some form of medical care in the prior 12 months because they could not afford it
- 43 percent of respondents reported that they could not afford to pay for a major medical expense out of pocket, and 34 percent reported that it is only somewhat likely that they could afford to pay
- 24 percent of respondents experienced what they described as a major unexpected medical expense that they had to pay out of pocket in the prior 12 months

Introduction

In September 2013, the Federal Reserve Board's Division of Consumer and Community Affairs conducted the Survey of Household Economics and Decisionmaking (SHED).

The SHED was conducted to capture a snapshot of the financial and economic well-being of U.S. households, as well as to monitor their recovery from the recent recession and identify any risks to their financial stability. It further collected information on households that was not readily available from other sources or was not available in combination with other variables of interest. The survey was designed in consultation with Federal Reserve System staff and outside academics with relevant research backgrounds.

The SHED provides a nationally representative snapshot of the economic situation of households in the United States at the time of the survey, as well their perspective on financial conditions in the recent past and expectations for conditions in the near future.

The survey contains questions on a range of topics, including

Table 1. Key survey response statistics: Main interview

Number sampled from main survey	Qualified completes	Completion rate
6,912	4,134	59.8%

- the personal finances of households;
- housing and living arrangements;
- credit access and behavior;
- education and student debt;
- savings;
- retirement; and
- health-related expenses.

Survey Background

The SHED was designed by Board staff and administered by GfK, an online consumer research company, on behalf of the Board. The questions included in the survey were designed to better illuminate the activities, experiences, and attitudes of individual consumers and households as they experienced their financial lives. In particular, several questions were included throughout the survey to better understand how households fared financially through the Great Recession and its aftermath, as well as their expectations regarding their households' future financial well-being. The SHED questions were designed to complement and augment the existing base of knowledge from other data sources, including the Board's own Survey of Consumer Finances (SCF).[1] In most cases, original questions were asked of respondents, although occasionally questions mirrored those from other surveys in order to provide direct comparisons and understand how certain variables interact with others.

The survey was conducted using a sample of adults ages 18 and over from KnowledgePanel®, a proprietary, probability-based web panel of more than 50,000 individuals from randomly sampled households. The sample is designed to be representative of the U.S. population. After pretesting, the data collection for the survey began on September 17, 2013, and concluded on October 4, 2013. As shown in table 1, e-mails were sent to 6,912 randomly selected members of KnowledgePanel resulting in 4,134 completed surveys and yielding a final stage completion rate of 59.8 percent. The respondents completed the survey in approximately 19 minutes (median time). Further details on the survey methodology are included in appendix 1.

As is the case with all surveys, some cautions in interpreting the survey results are prudent. Although the survey was designed to be nationally representative, some degree of selection bias is possible nonetheless (see appendix 1). Further, the results are all self-reported, and respondents' knowledge and memory may not always be completely accurate when answering survey questions. In anticipation of this challenge, certain questions were designed to avoid the appearance of false precision. For example, the survey could have asked respondents what their credit score was, but expectations were modest that many consumers would actually know the precise answer. Rather, the survey asked, "If you had to guess, how would you rate your current credit score?"; then it offered a range of imprecise but nonetheless meaningful options ranging from Poor to Excellent. In this way, the survey anticipated that typical respondents may have some limitations on their ability to precisely know and remember the answers to certain questions. Readers of the survey results are encouraged to keep these limitations in mind.

The following sections of this report summarize key findings from the SHED. The numbers cited in this report are derived from the Board survey unless otherwise noted. All data were weighted to yield estimates for the U.S. adult population. Only a subset of questions asked in the SHED are discussed in the report; however, the complete survey questionnaire is summarized in appendix 2. The responses to all the survey questions are presented in appendix 3 in the order that the questions were asked of respondents.

In general, the responses to the questions are discussed with reference to the entire population. However, for certain areas of inquiry where variation by demographic or socioeconomic factors may be anticipated, the responses are disaggregated by these factors and corresponding discussion is provided. For instance, the section on retirement planning includes a discussion of the role played by the respondents' ages. Given historic differences in racial lending patterns, the discussion of access to credit includes a discussion of variation by race/ethnicity. A table of summary statistics for the respondents' demographics is provided as table C.101. Cross-tabulations for additional questions by demographic and socioeconomic variations are available in an online appendix adjacent to the report at www.federalreserve.gov.

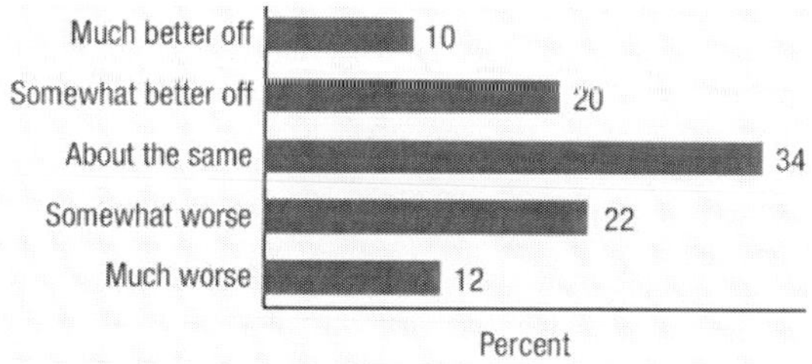

Note: Here and in subsequent figures, totals may not add to 100 percent due to rounding and question non-response.

Figure 1. Compared to five years ago, are you better off, worse off, or the same financially?

HOUSEHOLD ECONOMIC WELL-BEING

The survey asked households how they were faring, generally and in some specific ways, and also asked about how they were faring relative to several years ago.

Current Situation versus Five Years Ago

When asked how they were currently managing financially, 23 percent of respondents reported that they were "living comfortably," while 37 percent reported that they were "doing okay." A further 25 percent reported that they were "just getting by" financially, and the remaining 13 percent indicated that they were "finding it difficult to get by."

The vast majority of households also appear to be living within their means, with 38 percent reporting that they spent less than their income over the course of 2012 and an additional 38 percent reporting that their spending was equal to their income. Only 22 percent reported that they had spent more than their income. (Given that over half of respondents report having saved some money in 2012, a significant fraction of those reporting that their spending was equal to their income may be deducting savings through pension or 401(k) plans at work from their income before comparing it to their spending.)

Box 1. Household Responses to the Great Recession

Among the motivating factors for conducting the Survey of Household Economics and Decisionmaking was obtaining a better understanding of the challenges and decisions facing households as a result of the Great Recession and its aftermath. Some questions ask survey respondents to compare their present state to that in 2008, a point in time five years prior to the survey, and at the onset of the recession.1 For these types of questions, inferences can be made about the possible influence of the recession, but causation cannot be known with any certainty.

Survey respondents were also asked some specific questions about actions that they took and directly attribute to the recession. When asked, "Did you delay any major expenses or purchases because of the recession that began in 2008?," 42 percent said they had. Of those people, foregoing a vacation (67 percent) was the most common action cited. Other actions commonly cited by those who said they had delayed a major expense were buying a car (57 percent), making home improvements (44 percent), buying a major appliance (31 percent), or buying a home (20 percent). Five percent reported other expenses foregone. (Respondents could cite more than one delayed expense.)

The survey also asked, "Did you delay any major life decisions because of the recession that began in 2008?" Eighteen percent of people said they had. Of those people, buying a home was far and away the most common decision delayed (45 percent). Other decisions mentioned were moving to a new city or state (34 percent), changing jobs (21 percent), having a child (18 percent), retirement (16 percent), and marriage (15 percent). Another 9 percent cited other major life decisions that were delayed.

The survey indicates that many households have been providing assistance to one another during periods of financial distress. When asked about providing or receiving financial assistance to/from friends or family members, 22 percent of respondents said they had received such help since 2008, and 34 percent said they had provided such help during that time.

[1] The National Bureau of Economic Research finds that the recession officially began in December 2007.

Although majorities of individuals report doing okay or being financially comfortable and most individuals are living within their means, a number of respondents report living with others in order to save money. For instance, among the 16 percent of respondents who live with their adult children, their extended family, or a roommate, a little more than half say they are doing so to save money, and 73 percent would move out on their own if they could afford to do so.

When asked to compare their current financial situation to their financial situation five years prior, 34 percent reported doing somewhat or much worse financially, 34 percent reported doing about the same financially, and 30 percent reported that they were either somewhat or much better off (figure 1). Given that respondents were being asked to compare their incomes to 2008, when the United States was in the depths of the financial crisis, the fact that over twothirds of respondents reported being the same or worse off financially highlights the uneven nature of the recovery. (For a discussion of how households responded to the recession, see box 1.)

Financial Expectations and Stability

Expectations among most individuals in the U.S. adult population were that their incomes will be stable over the coming 12 months, with 61 percent reporting that they expected their total income to stay about the same as it had been over the prior 12 months, 21 percent believing it would be higher, and 16 percent believing it would be lower. A significant fraction of respondents (30 percent) reported that their household's income for 2012 was lower than what they would consider "normal" (figure 2). Of the 30 percent who view their 2012 income as below "normal," about half were not optimistic about their incomes recovering quickly. Among these respondents, 28 percent expected their income in the next 12 months to decline, while only 20 percent expected their income to increase in the next 12 months (table 2).

The survey also asked questions to better understand how steady and predictable households' income streams are. While two-thirds of respondents reported that their income is roughly the same from month to month, 21 percent said that they occasionally experience months with unusually high or low incomes, and 10 percent said that their income varies quite a bit from month to month. For those whose income varies, 42 percent reported that it was due to an irregular work schedule, and 15 percent said it was due to periods of unemployment. This was followed by bonuses and seasonal employment, which were each cited as reasons for month-to-month income variance by 12 percent of respondents. Of the 42 percent with an irregular work schedule, 58 percent worked full time, 30 percent worked part time, and 11 percent were self-employed.

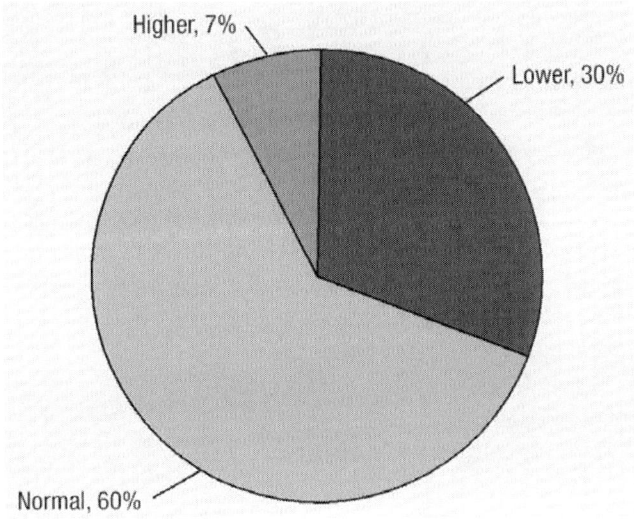

Figure 2. Was your total household income in 2012 higher or lower than what you would expect in a normal year?

Table 2. During the next 12 months, do you expect your total income to be higher or lower than in the previous 12 months? (by whether 2012 income was higher or lower than normal)
Percent, except as noted

	Lower	About the same	Higher
2012 income lower than normal	27.9	51.5	19.8
2012 income was normal	10.2	68.3	20.7
2012 income higher than normal	20.8	46.4	31.0
Overall	16.1	60.5	20.7
Total number of respondents			**4,134**

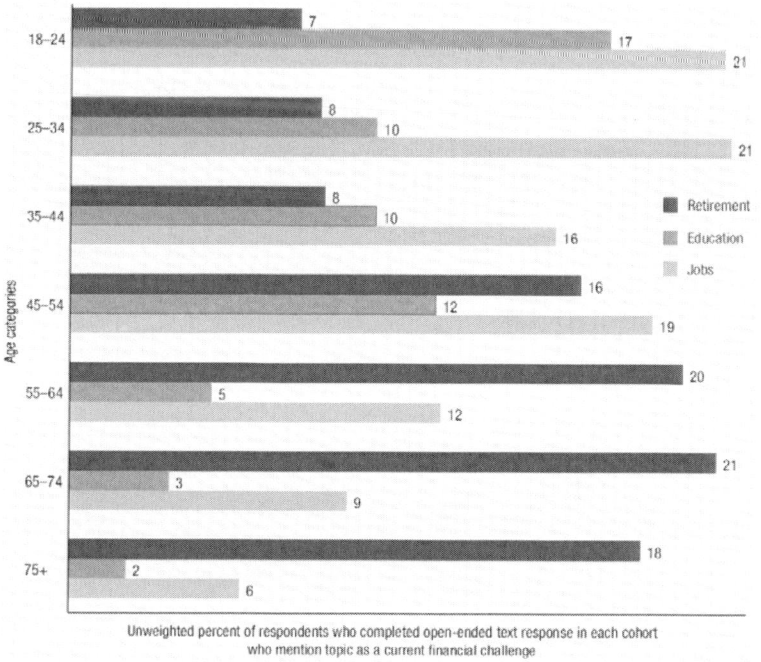

Figure 3. Most frequently cited concerns about retirement, college, and employment in open-ended text responses (by age).

Self-Reported Financial Challenges

In addition to asking specific questions about their financial situation, the survey invited respondents to describe their current financial challenges and economic concerns in their own words. About 45 percent chose an option labeled "none." This group may include some people who had no concerns and others who simply chose not to provide an answer. The remaining 55 percent of respondents provided some response to the open-ended question. These responses underwent text analysis in order to identify broad themes under which the respondents' financial challenges and economic concerns could be grouped.

Among the most prominent themes to emerge from the text analysis of the open-ended question were retirement, education, and employment.[2] Among those who opted to describe their financial challenges and concerns, there were differences by age cohort in the frequency with which each of these themes was mentioned (figure 3). Not surprisingly, the frequency of retirement concerns was highest among the older age cohorts. Of the respondents ages 45 or older who provided a text response, 19 percent described retirement concerns. This compares to just 8 percent with similar concerns among those under age 45. In contrast, the younger to mid-age cohorts had the highest frequency counts for concerns regarding college and education. Respondents also expressed high levels of concern regarding jobs and employment across all cohorts of working-age individuals. This concern was particularly acute among those ages 18 to 24 and 25 to 34, where 21 percent of each cohort reported concerns about jobs and employment. However, high levels of employment concerns were also prevalent among those ages 35 to 44 and those ages 45 to 54.

HOUSING AND HOUSEHOLD LIVING ARRANGEMENTS

Since housing is an important factor in most households' financial equation, the SHED posed a series of housing-related questions to survey participants. The survey included questions meant to increase understanding of how housing choices and experiences may have changed coming out of the recent recession.

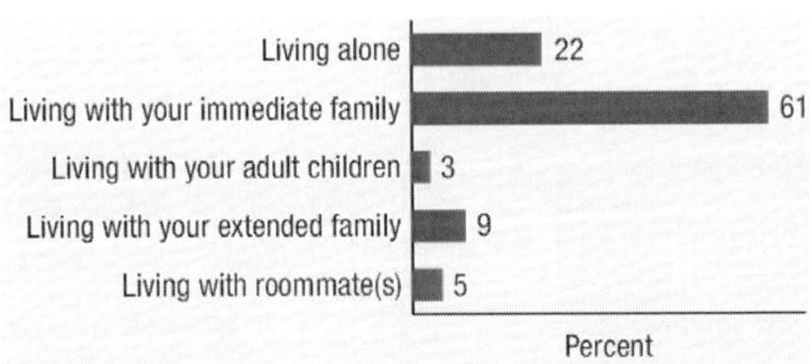

Figure 4. Which one of the following best describes your living arrangement?

In terms of their living arrangements, 22 percent of respondents reported living alone; the majority (61 percent) resided with their immediate family (figure 4).

According to the survey, 58 percent of all respondents owned their home in 2013, 32 percent rented, and 9 percent neither owned their home nor paid rent. Restricting the sample to heads of household only, the share who owned their home increased to 66 percent, which matches the Census estimate for the same period.[3] Among those who did not currently own a home, 6 percent had owned a home in the prior 12 months. The share of household heads who reported renting was 31 percent, and only 3 percent reported that they neither owned their home nor paid rent.

Renters

About one-third of households reported renting their home. The average renter paid $830 in monthly rent, while the median renter paid $700. Renters were asked to give all reasons for renting rather than owning their home, with the most common responses being that they can't afford a down payment to buy a home (45 percent), can't qualify for a mortgage (29 percent), find it more convenient to rent (24 percent), or find it cheaper to rent than own (23 percent). Almost 10 percent of renters indicated that they are currently looking to buy a home. The fact that 59 percent cited down-payment challenges, inability to obtain a mortgage, and/or reported that they were currently looking to buy as their reason for renting seems to indicate that a sizeable percentage of renters would ultimately prefer to own a home were it possible for them to do so. Others who cited convenience or affordability as their reasons to rent seemed to signal a preference for renting based on its own advantages.

The reasons that respondents cited for why they rent rather than own their home varied by age in several notable ways (figure 5). Among renters, those ages 18 to 29 were far more likely to indicate that they plan on moving in the near future (29 percent) than those in other age groups, and were the most likely to indicate that they can't afford the down payment (49 percent). Those ages 45 to 59 were the most likely to cite their inability to qualify for a mortgage as the reason for renting (41 percent), while those ages 60 and over simply prefer to rent (34 percent).

Over 50 percent of renters indicated that they had to cut back on spending to some degree over the prior 12 months in order to pay their rent, with 17 percent indicating that they had to cut spending back by "a lot."

Homeowners

Nearly 60 percent of respondents said they owned their home. Among homeowners at the time of the survey, 68 percent had a mortgage, and among mortgage holders, 21 percent also had a home equity line of credit. The average homeowner had purchased the home in 1998, while the median owner had bought the home in 2002.

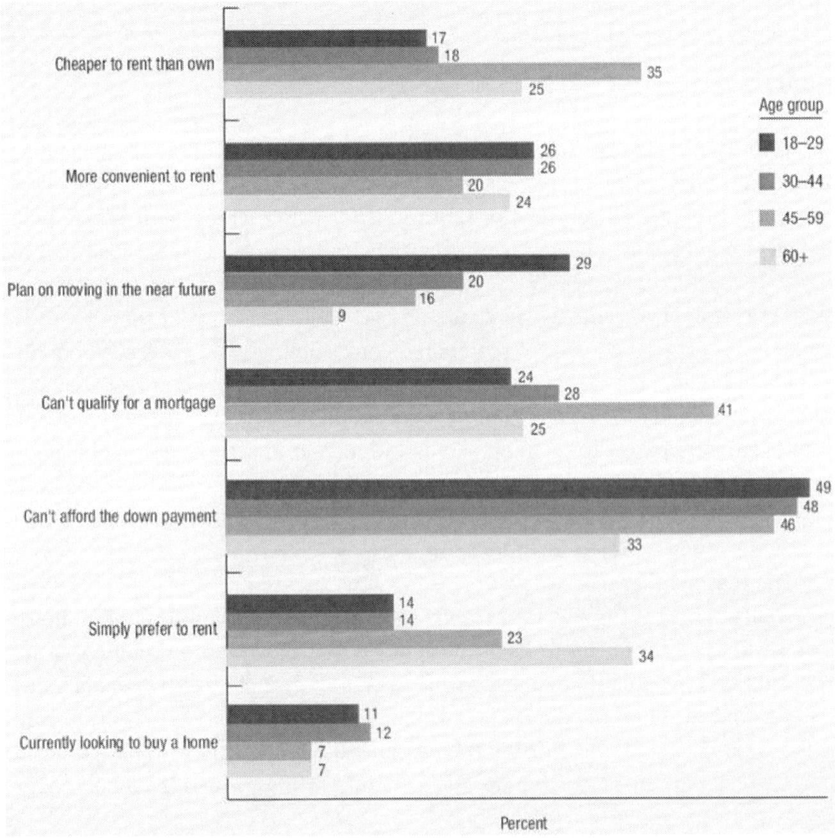

Figure 5. Reason(s) for renting rather than owning your home? (by age).

Nationally, home values have varied greatly in recent years. The SHED asked respondents who were homeowners about the perceived value of their own homes and how they believe those values have changed over time. When asked to compare the current value of their home to the value five years prior (2008), 45 percent of homeowners said that the value of their home was now lower, while 20 percent said that the value had stayed the same, and 27 percent said that the home now had a higher value. Eight percent said that they didn't know how or whether the value of their home had changed.

Most homeowners expected home values in their neighborhood to increase over the next 12 months, with 14 percent expecting values to increase by more than 5 percent and 26 percent expecting values to go up by less than 5 percent. Thirty-seven percent of homeowners expected the value of homes in their neighborhood to remain about the same over the coming 12 months, while less than 10 percent expected homes to decrease in value.

The depressed house prices appeared to prevent some homeowners from listing or selling their homes. When asked if they wanted to sell their home or had tried to sell their home over the prior 12 months, 9 percent of homeowners said they had kept their home off the market despite wanting to sell, and 2 percent said that they had listed their home but had been unable to sell it. In nearly three-quarters of cases, the current market value of the home was cited as the reason for not listing or selling the home.

HOUSEHOLD CREDIT BEHAVIOR AND PERCEPTIONS OF CONSUMER CREDIT AVAILABILITY

The financial crisis resulted in a general tightening of credit policies by financial institutions. The SHED asked several questions pertaining to the demand for credit by respondents in 2013. Based on the results of the survey, just under one-third of the U.S. adult population had applied for some type of credit in the prior 12 months (figure 6). An additional 15 percent reported that they had completely put off applying for credit because they thought they would be denied. After applying for credit, one-third were turned down or given less credit than they applied for, including 29 percent who were denied credit at least once (table 3).

Among those who did apply for credit in the prior 12 months, 26 percent also reported that they put off a separate credit application during the same time period because they thought they might be turned down.

Table 3. In the past 12 months, has each of the following happened to you? Percent, except as noted

	Yes	No
Denied credit	29.1	67.8
Offered less credit than applied for	14.9	81.2
Number of respondents		**1,359**

Note: Among those who reported having applied for credit in prior 12 months (33 percent of survey respondents).

Mortgages

Respondents are reasonably confident in their ability to obtain a mortgage if they were to apply for one.

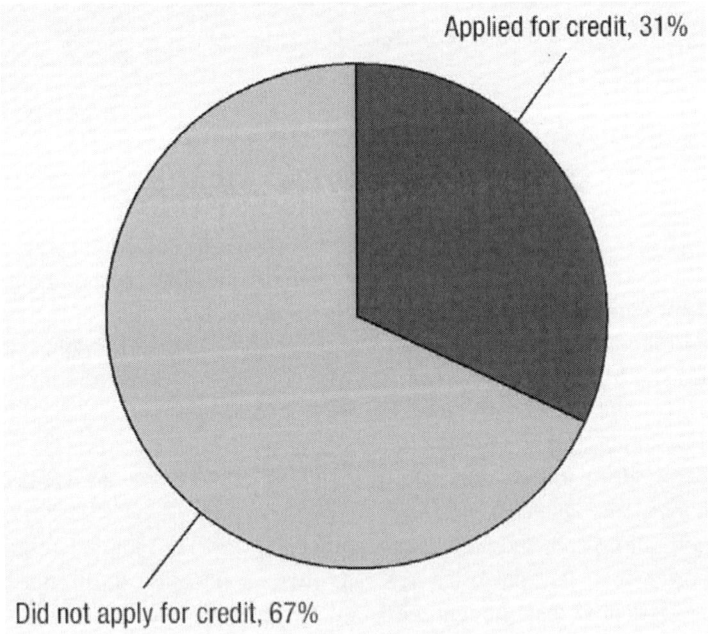

Figure 6. In the past 12 months, have you applied for any credit?

Table 4. If you applied for a mortgage today, how confident are you that your application would be approved? (by race and ethnicity) Percent, except as noted

Race/ethnicity	Confident	Not confident	Don't Know
White, non-Hispanic	57.3	27.0	14.2
Black, non-Hispanic	37.7	32.6	28.0
Other, non-Hispanic	54.5	22.8	21.9
Hispanic	42.2	37.2	18.3
2+ races, non-Hispanic	48.7	35.6	15.7
Overall	52.5	29.0	16.9
Total number of respondents			**4,134**

Table 5. If you applied for credit or a loan today (other than a mortgage), how confident are you that your application would be approved? (by race and ethnicity) Percent, except as noted

Race/ethnicity	Very confident	Somewhat confident	Not confident	Don't know
White, non-Hispanic	48.2	19.5	19.5	11.2
Black, non-Hispanic	20.8	24.5	28.0	24.5
Other, non-Hispanic	41.2	21.8	19.6	16.5
Hispanic	26.5	27.2	30.7	13.9
2+ races, non-Hispanic	36.9	18.3	30.8	14.0
Overall	41.2	21.3	22.3	13.6
Total number of respondents				**4,134**

Just over a third of all respondents were very confident that their mortgage application would be approved should they decide to apply, while 19 percent were somewhat confident. Twenty-nine percent of respondents were not confident that their mortgage application would be approved, and 17 percent simply did not know if it would be approved. Among those who were either somewhat or not confident that their application would be approved, 21 percent said they would be very likely to apply for a mortgage should it become easier to get approved for a mortgage, and 28 percent would be somewhat likely to apply.

The survey sheds some light on the extent to which race and ethnicity continue to be points of divergence when it comes to perceived access to credit. More specifically, the survey finds that experiences with access to, and expectations about, credit do vary. For instance, confidence in one's ability to obtain a mortgage differs substantially by race/ethnicity. Among non-Hispanic whites, 57 percent were confident that they would be approved for a mortgage should they apply, relative to 42 percent of Hispanics and 38 percent of non-Hispanic blacks (table 4). The reason for the gap in confidence between whites and minorities also differs by race/ethnicity. For Hispanics, this difference is largely driven by the share who report that they are not confident that their application would be approved (37 percent versus 27 percent for whites), while for blacks it is driven by the significant share who don't know if they would be approved (28 percent versus 14 percent for whites).

That said, since race/ethnicity is correlated with numerous other factors that may affect confidence in one's ability to obtain a mortgage, regression analysis was used to control for these other characteristics. The differences in confidence between whites and blacks and between whites and Hispanics are both statistically significant in a probit regression that also controls for age, income, gender, employment, and marital status, but no longer statistically significant when also controlling for education. This suggests that other factors such as racial and ethnic differences in education levels are important for fully understanding the question about confidence.

Credit Cards

The majority of respondents with credit cards reported that they pay off their balances in full each month (57 percent). Among the remaining 43 percent who revolve their credit card balances, 82 percent had been charged interest on their balance at some time in the prior 12 months. Also, among those who revolved their balance, 53 percent had made only the minimum payment, 42 percent had carried a balance using a low-interest rate balance transfer offer, and 12 percent had gotten a cash advance from their credit card at some point in the preceding 12 months.

As was the case for mortgage credit, access to a credit card differs substantially by race/ethnicity. Just 20 percent of non-Hispanic whites do not have at least one credit card, compared to 47 percent of non-Hispanic blacks and 30 percent of Hispanics. Respondents' confidence in their ability to get approved for credit also varied by race/ethnicity (table 5). As was the case for confidence that one's mortgage application would be approved, these differences in confidence between whites and blacks and between whites and Hispanics remain statistically significant when including many control variables but were no longer significant after also controlling for education levels. In the aggregate, these results suggest that race/ethnicity are still important factors when understanding consumers' experiences accessing and thinking about credit, but that the correlation between race/ethnicity and perceived access to credit may largely be a factor of other variables, such as education, that are correlated with race/ethnicity and credit.

SAVINGS BEHAVIOR

The survey asked a number of questions about respondents' general savings behavior, spending priorities, and ability to withstand significant financial disruptions. In general, the results demonstrate that many households are saving and want to save or pay down debt, although others struggle to maintain a financial safety net.

Saving and Spending

When asked what portion of their 2012 income was set aside as savings, a majority (55 percent) of survey respondents reported saving at least some part of their income. The average percentage of income reported saved among all respondents was 9 percent; however, the median was much lower (2 percent), and 45 percent of respondents reported that they did not save any portion of their income in 2012.[4] Of those respondents who did save, the average amount saved was 16 percent, with the median being 10 percent.

The amount that individuals reported saving is correlated with age: younger individuals reported saving a larger fraction of their incomes than older individuals, at statistically significant levels. Respondents ages 18 to 29 reported saving an average of 11 percent of their income; each of the other age groups (30–44, 45–59, and 60 or over) reported saving an average of 8 percent.

Relationships with financial institutions are highly correlated with saving, though causation is not clear: it could be that those who want to save are more likely to open accounts to do so, or that those who already have accounts simply find it easier to then save as a result. Respondents with a checking, savings, or money market account reported much higher levels of saving in 2012 than those without an account. Of the 90 percent of respondents with these accounts, the average percentage of income saved was 9 percent.[5] Of the remaining 10 percent of respondents who did not have a checking, savings, or money market account (the "unbanked"), only one in five (18 percent) reported saving any part of their income. For the unbanked, the average amount reported saved was 3 percent.

Respondents who reported saving some part of their income were asked to select all of the applicable reasons for why they were saving (table 6). The top reasons for saving were for their retirement (58 percent), unexpected expenses (53 percent), and "just to save" (49 percent).

According to the survey, respondents said that they were currently emphasizing paying down debt and saving. Just over half of respondents regularly set aside part of any income they received in a separate savings account. As another gauge of respondents' spending and saving priorities, the survey included a hypothetical question asking people how they would allocate the money if they unexpectedly received an extra $1,000 in income. Just under half reported that they would spend at least some of this windfall. Overall, the average hypothetical spending was $227, the average hypothetical saving was $395, and the average hypothetical amount allocated to paying down debt (a form of saving) was $377. Only about 7 percent said that they would spend the entire $1,000. Just over 20 percent reported that they would use the entire $1,000 to pay down debt, while another 17 percent reported that they would save the entire $1,000.

Table 6. Which of the following categories, if any, are you saving money for? Percent, except as noted

Category	Yes	No
Retirement	58.0	42.0
Unexpected expenses	52.6	47.4
Just to save	49.1	50.9
Pay off debts	26.5	73.5
Your children	20.5	79.5
Major appliance	20.4	79.6
Education	17.9	82.2
Home purchase	13.0	87.0
Leave inheritance or charitable donation	10.6	89.4
Total number of respondents		**2,270**

Note: Among those who report saving some part of their income.

Table 7. Have you set aside emergency or rainy day funds that would cover your expenses for 3 months? (by age)
Percent, except as noted

Age categories	Yes	No
18–29	33.2	63.0
30–44	32.6	63.6
45–59	34.4	64.1
60+	56.3	41.7
Overall	39.4	57.9
Total number of respondents		**1,998**

Emergency Savings

In addition to the general questions about saving, the survey asked respondents several questions to better understand their ability to withstand emergencies, such as the loss of a job, extended illness, or major unexpected expense. The responses varied depending on which specific question was asked, but in general the results indicate that many households appear ill-prepared for emergencies.

Half of respondents were asked if they had set aside an emergency or rainy day fund that would cover three months of expenses. The other half were asked a broader question, "If you were to lose your main source of income (e.g., job, government benefits), could you cover your expenses for 3 months by borrowing money, using savings, selling assets, or borrowing from friends/family?" Among those asked if they had a rainy day fund, 39 percent said yes, while 56 percent of those asked the broader question said yes. This difference may suggest that some respondents expect to rely on debt or their personal social networks as a safety net in an emergency in the absence of sufficient personal savings.

Despite having less time to have built up savings, young respondents reported similar frequencies as older working-age respondents of having rainy day funds. Among respondents under the age of 60, the presence of rainy day funds does not vary significantly by age, although individuals ages 60 or older are more likely than others to have them (table 7).

Table 8. Could you cover your expenses for 3 months by borrowing money, using savings, selling assets, or borrowing from friends/family? (by age)
Percent, except as noted

Age categories	Yes	No
18–29	53.9	42.5
30–44	48.0	49.9
45–59	53.4	45.0
60+	66.6	31.8
Overall	55.6	42.2
Total number of respondents		**2,136**

The results by age were similar when respondents were asked the broader question including borrowing and selling, although the numbers were higher across the board. For respondents under the age of 60, about one-third had rainy day funds, but about half said they could "cover expenses," including by borrowing. For those over the age of 60, a bit more than half (56 percent) had rainy day funds, but two-thirds responded affirmatively to the broader question about covering expenses (table 8).

The prior questions asked respondents about a serious and prolonged (three-month) disruption in their financial lives. To get a more nuanced understanding of how financially fragile various households may be, the survey also asked a similar question—but about a disruption on a much smaller scale. Respondents were asked how they would pay for an emergency expense that came along and cost $400. Just under half (48 percent) reported that they could fairly easily handle such an expense, paying for it entirely using cash, money currently in their checking/savings account, or on a credit card that they would pay in full at their next statement. The remainder indicated that such an expense would be more challenging to handle: respondents indicated that they simply could not cover the expense (19 percent); would have to sell something (9 percent); or would have to rely on one or more means of borrowing to pay for at least part of the expense, including paying with a credit card that they pay off over time (17 percent), borrowing from friends or family (12 percent), or using a payday loan (4 percent).

The Great Recession appears to have had a significant effect on respondents' tapping into their savings, including those specifically set aside for a rainy day. Sixty-one percent of respondents said that their household had savings prior to 2008. Of that group, 32 percent said that they had used up some of their savings in the intervening five years, 12 percent had used up nearly all of their savings, and 13 percent had used up all of their savings. Overall, the survey results indicate that a great number of households want to save, many are doing so, but that others indicate some measure of significant financial vulnerability to unexpected events. This has potentially increased in recent years as a result of eroded savings.

Education, Student Loans, and Job Readiness

The survey asked respondents several questions about their educational experience and their financing for it, when applicable. They were also asked about their perceived readiness for the jobs of today and the future.

Student Loans

According to the survey, 16 percent of respondents have some debt associated with their education, 7 percent have debt from paying for a spouse's education, 6 percent have debt from a child's education, and less than 1 percent have debt from a grandchild's education (table 9).[6] Overall, 24 percent of respondents have education debt for themselves, someone else, or a combination. Among those who have at least some education beyond a high school degree, the percent with student loan debt is higher, with 22 percent reporting debt for their own education and 31 percent reporting education debt for themselves or someone else.[7] Among those with each type of education debt, the average amount people reported owing for their own education was $25,750, with a median value of $13,000 (table 10). The amounts for spouses' education was similar, though debt loads for children's education was substantially lower. For those with education debt (for themselves and/or others), the average combined amount was $27,840, and the median amount was $15,000. (The median amount of education debt is consistently lower than the average amount of education debt, as the average value of education debt is skewed upwards by a small number of people with a substantial amount of debt.) Just over half of those with debt for their own education indicated that they were currently making payments on at least one education loan, while 34 percent indicated that they had one or more loan in deferment or forbearance. Respondents indicated significant challenges making their payments. Eighteen percent of those who owe money for their own education indicated that they were behind on payments for their own education debt or reported that they had loans in collections. Those who were married or living with a partner were less likely to report that their own education loan was in collections (5 percent) than those who were single and never married (11 percent). However, these effects may be partially attributable to age differences by marital status.

Table 8. Could you cover your expenses for 3 months by borrowing money, using savings, selling assets, or borrowing from friends/family? (by age) Percent, except as noted

Age categories	Yes	No
18–29	53.9	42.5
30–44	48.0	49.9
45–59	53.4	45.0
60+	66.6	31.8
Overall	55.6	42.2
Total number of respondents		**2,136**

Table 9. Do you currently owe any money or have any loans that you used to pay for the education of any of the categories of people below? Percent, except as noted

	Yes	No
Your own education	15.8	68.6
Spouse/partner's education	7.5	62.6
Child's education	5.7	59.5
Grandchild's education	0.6	52.5
Total number of respondents		**4,134**

Table 10. Mean and median current amount owed on student loan debt incurred (by recipient of education)

	Mean	Median	Respondents
Your own education	$25,750	$13,000	514
Spouse/partner's education	$24,593	$12,000	237
Child's education	$14,923	$ 8,000	233
Grandchild's education	$16,090	$ 6,000	20
Combined amount	**$27,840**	**$15,000**	**849**

Note: Among those who currently owe any money or have any loans for each education category and report a positive amount owed.

Table 11. Overall, how would you say the lifetime financial benefits of your most recent educational program compare to the lifetime financial costs to you of this education? (by degree completion) Percent, except as noted

	Benefits outweigh costs	About the same	Costs outweigh benefits
Did not complete degree	22.9	20.6	56.5
Completed degree	41.5	20.1	38.1
Still enrolled in the program	59.3	23.1	17.1
Total number of respondents			**566**

Note: Among those who currently owe any money or have any loans for their own education and reported their completion status. Responses for "much larger benefits" and "somewhat larger benefits" are aggregated together, as are responses for "much smaller benefits" and "somewhat smaller benefits."

For those who reported the amount of monthly payments on loans for their own education, the average monthly payment was $245, with a median value of $160. For those making monthly payments for their spouse's education, the average monthly payment was $242 ($200 median), and for those making debt payments for a child's education the average monthly payment was $279 ($164 median).

Nearly half of respondents who are currently making payments on their education debt reported that the costs of servicing this debt impacts other spending decisions. Across all respondents making payments, for themselves or others, 11 percent indicated that they had to cut back on their spending by "a lot" in the prior 12 months in order to make their education debt payments, while an additional 35 percent indicated that they had to cut back on their spending by "a little" in order to make their payments.

Among those respondents who borrowed to pay for their own education, 48 percent indicated that they completed the program they had enrolled in, while 27 percent were still enrolled. Nearly one in four—24 percent—had dropped out before completion. Focusing on those who are making payments on their own education debt, 17 percent of those who did not complete their program of study had to cut back on their spending by "a lot" in the prior 12 months in order to make their payments. This amount is almost twice as much as among those who had completed their program (9 percent). Moreover, 37 percent of those who did not complete their program had to cut back by "a little" in order to make their payments, compared with 30 percent of those who completed their program. Thus, in total, 54 percent of those who did not complete their education program had to cut back on their spending in order to service their student debt, compared with 39 percent of those who completed their education.

Respondents appear to be split on whether the financial benefits they have received from their education outweigh the cost of that education. Forty-two percent of respondents with education debt for themselves felt that the lifetime financial benefits from their education outweighed the costs, while 37 percent said that the financial costs outweighed the benefits. Those who did not complete their program of study were far more likely than others to say that the financial benefits of their education were much smaller than the cost (table 11).

Educational Field and Financial Well-Being

Respondents with education debt were asked about the major or field of study for which the debt was used to pay. The sample sizes by any one major are too small to yield statistically valid results, so particular caution should be taken in estimating the perceived value of any single field or major. Nevertheless, in aggregate, the results indicate that the respondent's field of study influenced the perceived value of the lifetime financial benefits expected from the education program relative to the financial costs incurred. For example, 63 percent of those who majored in engineering felt the financial benefits of their education outweighed the costs, while only 26 percent of those majoring in computer or information sciences felt the same (table 12).

Type of Institution Attended and Financial Well-Being

Across various dimensions, the outcomes for those with education debt varied by the type of institution they attended; however, it should be noted that the results presented here do not control for any differences in the characteristics of borrowers across institution type. Additionally, these results only reflect the respondents who have education debt, and they do not reflect respondents who attended a postsecondary institution but did not take out debt or have completely paid off the debt.[8]

As shown in table 13, the amount of current debt owed for respondents' own education was highest at private not-for-profit four-year institutions, with an average amount of $39,501 and median amount of $20,000. This was followed by private for-profit four-year institutions, with an average debt amount of $30,475 (median $19,900). Those with education debt who attended public four-year institutions owed less debt, with an average of $25,311 (median $15,000).

Although the level of education debt is highest for those who attended private not-for-profit four-year institutions, the median incomes of these respondents were higher as well. Among those reporting income, the median income among respondents who attended and completed programs at private nonprofit four-year colleges was $80,000, compared with $52,000 for those who completed programs at public four-year institutions and $40,000 for those who completed programs at private for-profit four-year colleges.

Table 12. Overall, how would you say the lifetime financial benefits of your most recent educational program compare to the lifetime financial costs to you of this education? (by educational field)
Percent, except as noted

Category of major	Benefits outweigh costs	About the same	Costs outweigh benefits
Humanities	31.8	16.4	51.8
Social/behavioral sciences	26.0	37.0	37.1
Life sciences	56.0	5.3	38.7
Physical sciences/math	40.4	12.0	47.6
Computer/information sciences	22.0	30.9	47.1
Engineering	63.3	17.5	18.1
Education	38.5	21.1	39.8
Business/management	43.1	22.0	34.9
Health	53.3	19.3	27.4
Law	49.9	9.2	40.9
Vocational/technical	51.5	18.7	29.9
Undeclared	10.9	29.6	54.6
Overall	42.0	18.3	36.7
Total number of respondents			**560**

Note: Among those who currently owe any money or have any loans for their own education and and reported their field of study. Responses for "much larger benefits" and "somewhat larger benefits" are aggregated together, as are responses for "much smaller benefits" and "somewhat smaller benefits."

Table 13. Mean and median current amount owed on student loan debt incurred for respondent's own education (by institution type)

Type of institution	Median	Mean	Standard deviation
Public, 4-year institution	$15,000	$25,311	$28,441
Private not-for-profit, 4-year	$20,000	$39,501	$46,018
Private for-profit, 4-year	$19,900	$30,475	$35,655
Public, 2-year	$ 7,000	$ 8,519	$ 5,968
Private for-profit, 2-year	$10,000	$11,937	$ 8,701
Overall	$15,000	$26,607	$33,927
Total number of respondents			**451**

Note: Among those who currently owe any money or have any loans for their own education and reported the school for which they most recently borrowed money.

The employment rates of respondents also varied by postsecondary institution type. The share of respondents reporting that they were either a paid employee or self-employed was highest among those who completed programs at private non-profit institutions (90 percent), with those who completed programs at public institutions (86 percent) and private for-profit colleges (74 percent) reporting somewhat lower values.

Among those with education debt who attended four-year institutions, respondents who attended private not-for-profit institutions were more likely to report that they completed their education (63 percent) than attendees of public (48 percent) and for-profit institutions (35 percent). Those who attended private not-for-profit institutions were also more likely to report that they were actively making payments on their education debt (68 percent) than those who attended public (54 percent) or for-profit (35 percent) institutions.

Ability to make payments also varies by institution type. Only 5 percent of those who attended four-year, private not-for-profit institutions reported that they are behind on their education loan payments, compared to 10 percent of those who attended public institutions and 23 percent of those who attended for-profit institutions. Similarly, no one who attended a private not-for-profit institution reported that one or more of their education loans were in collections, compared with 6 percent of those who attended public institutions and 13 percent of those who attended for-profit institutions. Deferment or forbearance were also far more common among those who attended for-profit institutions, with 59 percent reporting at least one loan currently in forbearance or deferment, compared with 35 percent of those who attended a public institution and 28 percent of those who attended a private not-for-profit institution.

Finally, perception of the lifetime financial benefits of the education compared with the costs among those who currently have education debt varied by type of institution attended. In general, those who attended a public college (either two-or four-year) reported the greatest perceived net benefits, followed by those who attended a private not-for-profit, four-year college, and then those who attended a for-profit college (either two-or four-year) (table 14).

Job Readiness

The survey also asked respondents questions meant to gauge their perception of their own readiness for the current and future job market. In general, the results paint a picture of confidence about education and work experience. Respondents were asked, "Thinking about your current education and work experience, how confident are you that you have the skills necessary to get the kinds of jobs you want now?" Thirty-nine percent said they were somewhat confident, and 27 percent said they were very confident, that they have the skills and experience to compete in today's job market (table 15). Only 18 percent said they were not confident.

When asked the same question, but this time thinking about the types of jobs respondents believed would be available 10 years down the road, confidence remained high. Thirty-nine percent said they were somewhat confident in their future competitiveness, and 23 percent said they were very confident. Again, about one-fifth (19 percent) said they were not confident.

When asked for all the reasons why they lacked confidence, needing additional education and needing additional job training were cited most frequently as the causes for concern, both for jobs now and for jobs in 10 years. For those concerned about current jobs, education was the most frequent response (49 percent), followed by job training (40 percent), while needing additional job training (48 percent) trumped needing further education (41 percent) as the most frequent cause of concern for jobs in 10 years. However, for both questions, skills being out of date, the rapidly changing job market, and a lack of availability of jobs they are qualified for were all cited as concerns by at least one-fifth of respondents who had expressed a lack of confidence.

Table 14. Overall, how would you say the lifetime financial benefits of your most recent educational program compare to the lifetime financial costs to you of this education? (by institution type)
Percent, except as noted

Type of institution	Benefits outweigh costs	About the same	Costs outweigh benefits
Public, 4-year institution	45.5	20.3	33.8
Private not-for-profit, 4-year	41.9	16.8	41.0
Private for-profit, 4-year	39.5	22.5	38.0
Public, 2-year	44.6	32.9	22.5
Private for-profit, 2-year	33.8	15.9	50.3
Overall	42.8	21.0	35.9
Total number of respondents			**473**

Note: Among those who currently owe any money or have any loans for their own education.

Table 15. How confident are you that you have the skills necessary to get the kinds of jobs you want?
Percent, except as noted

	Now	In 10 years
Very confident	27.3	23.2
Somewhat confident	39.2	38.8
Not confident	18.3	19.2
I am not currently in the workforce and I am not		
looking for a job	6.9	n/a
I do not expect to be working 10 years from now	n/a	8.0
Don't know	6.5	8.7
Total number of respondents		**2,864**

n/a Not applicable.

Retirement

In addition to present well-being, the SHED also asked questions that probed respondents' assessment of their future well-being, particularly as it pertains to retirement and financial preparations for retirement.

Planning for Retirement

When it comes to planning and saving for retirement, the survey results tell a somewhat cautionary tale. Although the long-term shift from defined-benefit (e.g., pension) to defined-contribution (e.g., 401(k)) plans places significant responsibilities on individuals to plan for their own retirement, only about one-fourth appear to be actively doing so.[9] Only 11 percent of respondents who are not currently retired report that they have given "a lot" of thought to financial planning for their retirement, while an additional 16 percent have given it "a fair amount" of thought. Nearly half of respondents (49 percent) said that they had thought only "a little" or "none at all" about financial planning for retirement. There is a modest difference in retirement planning by gender, with women being slightly more likely (28 percent) than men (23 percent) to report having given no thought to retirement planning.

As might be expected, the amount of thought given to retirement planning varies considerably by age (table 16). The proportion of those ages 18 to 29 who said they had given no thought at all to retirement planning was the highest of any age group, at 41 percent. However, even those closest to traditional retirement ages show only a modest level of planning: of those age 60 and over, only one-fifth said they had given "a lot" of thought to retirement planning, about the same percentage of that group who said they had given it no thought at all. Income also appears to be related to retirement planning. Of those with six-figure incomes, for instance, 22 percent reported that they had given financial planning for retirement "a lot" of thought, nearly double the rate of the overall population, while only 7 percent of those earning less than $25,000 said the same.

Table 16. How much thought have you given to the financial planning for your retirement? (by age)
Percent, except as noted

	18–29	**30–44**	**45–59**	**60+**	**Overall**
None at all	40.7	20.7	18.6	19.7	25.2
A little	27.3	26.1	20.1	19.0	23.8
Some	17.6	25.9	24.6	19.3	22.6
A fair amount	7.9	16.1	20.2	20.6	15.7
A lot	4.7	9.7	15.7	20.5	11.4
Total number of respondents					**3,163**

Note: Among those who are not currently retired.

Table 17. Which one of the following best describes your plan for retirement? (by age)
Percent, except as noted

	18–29	30–44	45–59	60+	Overall
I do not plan to retire	4.8	6.0	8.0	3.1	6.2
Work fewer hours as I get close to retirement	13.8	9.9	6.1	14.2	9.6
Retire from my current career, but then find a different full-time job	4.5	4.4	4.2	0.2	3.8
Retire from my current career, but then find a different part-time job	14.8	13.2	18.1	16.6	15.8
Retire from my current career, but then work for myself	10.0	10.6	10.4	6.1	9.9
Work full time until I retire, then stop working altogether	34.6	29.2	22.1	14.6	25.5
Keep working as long as possible	15.8	21.6	21.2	28.1	21.3
Other	0.9	3.7	9.8	16.4	7.2
Total number of respondents					**1,766**

Note: Among those who have given at least some thought to retirement.

This relationship between income and retirement planning is partially driven by respondents with higher incomes being more likely to be older and closer to retirement age. However, even after accounting for age, education, race/ethnicity, and other characteristics, higher income remains a significant predictor of greater planning for retirement.[10]

There are also differences in expectations for retirement among those who have planned for it. Among those who have given at least "some" thought to retirement, only a quarter anticipate that they will experience the traditional notion of retirement, which is working full time until a retirement date and then no longer working at all. Conversely, for just over one-fifth of this group, their "retirement plan" was to keep working as long as possible. An additional 6 percent of those who have thought about retirement do not think they will ever stop working. Many respondents plan to ease out of the labor force, with 16 percent planning to retire from their current career but then find a different part-time job, 10 percent planning to retire and then work for themselves, and an additional 4 percent planning to retire and then find a different full-time job.

The expectations for one's path to retirement vary considerably with age, with the expectation of traditional retirement shrinking as people approach traditional retirement ages (table 17). Thirty-five percent of those ages 18 to 29 reported that they expect to work full time until a set retirement date and then stop working altogether. This percentage declines steadily over the older age cohorts, until only 15 percent of those ages 60 and over expect to work full time until a set retirement date and then stop working altogether. Older respondents were more likely to have reported that they will either gradually reduce the hours they work as they approach retirement, or that they will retire from their current career and then find a part-time job. From this survey alone, it is not possible to know whether these differences reflect a change in desired outcome over time (with older adults perhaps realizing that they want to stay in the workforce longer than younger adults believe they will), an increased understanding of the financial challenges of full retirement, or simply intergenerational differences in attitude about retirement.

Responses to the question about the path to retirement also vary consistently by income, indicating that expectations around retirement are closely linked to financial circumstances. While 35 percent of those earning six figures reported that they intend to work full time until a retirement date and then stop working, only 15 percent of those earning less than $25,000 intend to do so. Similarly, 28 percent of those earning less than $25,000 indicated that they expect to "keep working as long as possible," while only 13 percent of those earning $100,000 or more said the same. Women were also more likely (25 percent) than men (18 percent) to expect to "keep working as long as possible."

For some individuals, a lack of financial planning for retirement may merely reflect a lack of interest in being retired. However, for others, a lack of preparedness for retirement may simply preclude it as an option—or spur difficult decisions in the future for those who do not plan to retire but are unable to stay in the workforce.

Saving for Retirement

The lack of preparedness is not signaled by a lack of planning alone. Many respondents, particularly those with limited incomes, indicated that they simply have few or no financial resources available for retirement. When asked what types of retirement savings or pension they have, 31 percent of those respondents who aren't yet retired reported that they have no retirement savings or pension whatsoever. For those with resources for retirement, respondents were allowed to indicate all the ways they were saving for retirement. The most commonly reported form of retirement savings is a defined contribution plan, such as a 401(k) or 403(b) plan, which 44 percent of people possess. Over a third (36 percent) of adults reported that they are eligible for Social Security Old-Age benefits, and 18 percent reported that they are covered by a traditional "defined benefit" pension through an employer.[11] Almost a quarter (23 percent) reported that they are saving for retirement using an individual retirement account (IRA), and the same proportion are saving for retirement outside of a formal retirement account (23 percent). Eleven percent of respondents indicated that they are saving for retirement utilizing real estate or land investments, which, for some, presumably includes tapping the equity of the home they own.

Table 18. What type(s) of retirement savings or pension do you (or your spouse/partner) have? (by age)
Percent, except as noted

	18–29	30–44	45–59	60+	Overall
No retirement savings or pension	50.5	27.8	23.0	15.4	30.9
Social Security Old-Age benefits	17.5	31.5	46.4	67.6	36.3
401(k), 403(b), thrift or other defined contribution pension plan through an employer	30.3	52.8	47.9	37.1	43.7
Defined benefit pension through an employer (i.e., pension based on a formula, your earnings, and years of service)	7.0	16.0	27.0	25.9	18.2
Individual Retirement Account (IRA)	11.2	23.5	29.2	31.9	23.0
Savings outside a retirement account (e.g., a brokerage account, savings account)	15.4	19.3	28.6	33.3	22.7
Real estate or land	4.4	8.9	16.2	20.5	11.3
Other	1.7	3.4	4.1	4.1	3.2
Total number of respondents					**3,163**

Note: Among those who are not currently retired.

As with retirement planning, patterns of retirement savings also differ substantially, and predictably, by age (table 18). For nearly every retirement savings category, the percentage of people reporting that they have that type of resource increases steadily with age. There is one notable exception. Holders of defined contribution plans, such as 401(k)s, are most common in the 30–44 age group, with percentages decreasing with older cohorts. This seeming anomaly may be driven by the fact that the most common of these types of plans were not available until the 1980s.

Similarly, nearly two-thirds of those ages 18 to 29 reported that they have no retirement savings or pension (including Social Security). This percentage declines steadily by age cohort. However, while the incidence of retirement savings increases with age, even among those ages 60 and over the percentage with no retirement savings is still striking: 15 percent of respondents in this group who are not yet retired reported having no retirement savings or pension, including Social Security. When Social Security is excluded as a form of retirement "savings," the share of respondents ages 60 and over with no retirement savings rises to 31 percent.

Even when respondents do have established retirement savings accounts, they do not necessarily treat such funds as untouchable. Seven percent of those with retirement savings reported that they had borrowed money from their retirement account during the preceding 12 months.

Moreover, 5 percent of those with such accounts reported that they had cashed out some of their retirement savings in the prior 12 months. (See box 2 for more on the interrelationship between retirement savings and other resources.)

BOX 2. LACK OF RETIREMENT SAVINGS AND OTHER FINANCIAL MEANS

Why do so many households have no retirement savings at all? Some of the respondents are simply younger people whose financial priorities do not yet include saving for retirement. But part of the story also seems to be one of financial fragility for some households, who lack retirement savings and also have little financial cushion at all. Over half (54 percent) of those with incomes under $25,000 reported having no retirement savings or pension, compared with 10 percent of those earning $100,000 or more.

Of those who reported that they had no retirement savings or pension, 67 percent also reported that they did not regularly set aside part of their income in some type of savings account, compared to 47 percent of the overall population. Similarly, of those without retirement resources, 86 percent also said they did not set aside emergency or rainy-day funds sufficient to cover their expenses for three months in an emergency, compared with 58 percent of the overall population.[1] It would appear that many of the nearly one-third of the population without any retirement resources also operate with a limited savings safety net.

[1] The question about emergency/rainy day funds was randomly asked of only half of respondents. Eighty-six percent of those who said they had no retirement savings or pension and were asked the question about rainy day funds reported that they had no such funds.

In addition to the differences by age in the types of retirement savings currently held, there are also differences in the expected approaches to paying for retirement. When it comes to Social Security, there are marked differences in expectations about coverage (table 19). Only 20 percent of those under age 30 reported that they anticipate that Social Security (technically, Social Security "Old-Age") benefits will be part of their plan to pay for expenses in retirement. This percentage steadily increased by age cohort, until 74 percent of those over age 60 reported expecting to include Social Security in their retirement plans. It is unclear whether these differences simply highlight the fact that older adults are likely to be thinking more actively about Social Security or represent diminishing levels of confidence among younger people about the future availability of Social Security benefits. Similarly, traditional defined-benefits pension plans are less common as an expected source of retirement funding among younger respondents. Twenty-nine percent of those ages 60 and older are counting on income from a defined-benefit pension, while only 7 percent of those ages 18 to 29 plan to pay for expenses using a defined-benefit pension.

Continued employment is expected to be a significant source of retirement income, as 24 percent of all respondents expect that they will continue working in some capacity to cover their expenses, and 9 percent expect their spouse to continue working. Just over 23 percent of people plan to rely on savings they hold outside formal retirement accounts to cover their expenses, while 22 percent plan to rely on their IRAs. Only a relatively small fraction of respondents plan to use income from real estate, the sale of a business, or help from family members in retirement. Perhaps as telling a number as any other is the following: when asked this question about how they and their spouse will pay for expenses in retirement, one-fourth of all respondents—and 14 percent of those ages 45 and older—chose "I don't know."

The Decision to Retire and Experiences in Retirement

The Great Recession appears to have adversely affected the retirement plans of a significant portion of the U.S. adult population. The respondents who had not retired and had given at least "some" thought to retirement were asked about their current retirement plans versus their retirement plans prior to 2008. One-third reported that they plan to retire at the same age as they had planned prior to 2008. A similar number (36 percent) said they now planned to retire at a later age than before the recession. This percentage was higher for those closest to traditional retirement ages: 41 percent of those ages 45 and over reported that they now planned to retire at a later date than they had before 2008. Only 5 percent of respondents who gave at least "some" thought to retirement now plan to retire sooner than they had prior to 2008, and almost a quarter reported that they were not thinking about retirement prior to 2008 and, thus, do not have a point of comparison.

As with other retirement expectations, there was variation across income groups in how the recession affected planned retirement age. As a group, those earning over $100,000 appeared to be relatively more insulated from the recession than other groups: 49 percent reported that their retirement age had not changed, relative to 33 percent of all respondents.

Table 19. How are you (and your spouse/partner) planning to pay for your expenses in retirement? (by age)
Percent, except as noted

	18–29	30–44	45–59	60+	Overall
Social Security Old-Age benefits	20.4	41.4	58.4	74.2	44.6
I will continue working	18.7	24.5	24.5	30.0	23.5
Spouse/partner will continue working	6.4	8.9	11.2	7.2	8.8

Table 19. How are you (and your spouse/partner) planning to pay for your expenses in retirement? (by age)
Percent, except as noted

	18–29	30–44	45–59	60+	Overall
Defined benefit pension from work (i.e., pension based on a formula, your earnings, and years of service)	7.3	16.1	26.8	29.0	18.5
401(k), 403(b), thrift or other defined contribution pension plan from work	31.6	46.0	43.5	30.2	39.7
Individual Retirement Account (IRA)	14.1	22.5	26.3	28.6	22.1
Savings outside a retirement account (e.g., a brokerage account, savings account)	19.3	23.3	24.9	29.2	23.4
Income from real estate or the sale of real estate	6.1	7.1	10.4	11.0	8.3
Income from a business or the sale of a business	4.6	3.7	3.1	4.5	3.9
Rely on children, grandchildren, or other family	4.6	1.9	2.6	1.7	2.8
I don't know	40.7	24.8	16.2	8.7	24.6
Other	1.1	2.4	4.8	5.6	3.1
Total number of respondents					**3,051**

Note: Among those who are not currently retired.

Table 20. What sources are you (and your spouse/partner) using to pay for your expenses in retirement?
Percent, except as noted

	Yes	No
Social Security Old-Age benefits	74.5	25.5
I have a job	5.8	94.2
My spouse/partner has a job	11.9	88.1
Defined benefit pension from work (i.e., pension based on a formula, your earnings, and years of service)	44.3	55.7

	Yes	No
401(k), 403(b), thrift or other defined contribution pension plan from work	18.5	81.5
Individual Retirement Account (IRA)	28.8	71.2
Savings outside a retirement account (e.g., a brokerage account, savings account)	31.6	68.4
Income from real estate or the sale of real estate	8.8	91.2
Income from a business or the sale of a business	2.6	97.4
Relying on children, grandchildren, or other family	1.9	98.1
Other	5.9	94.1
Total number of respondents		**971**

Note: Among those who are currently retired.

Those survey respondents who identified themselves as being currently retired were asked about their experiences in retirement and about how they manage their expenses. In terms of their path to retirement, a clear majority (58 percent) reported that they had followed the traditional model of working full time until they retired, and then stopped working altogether. (This is more than double the percent of the non-retired reporting that this is the path they expected to follow.)

However, many others followed less traditional paths. Fifteen percent had eased into retirement, working fewer hours as they approached their retirement date. Others continued to work at some point after retirement. Six percent had retired from their previous career but later worked a fulltime job, and 14 percent worked at a part-time job. Eight percent had retired from their previous career but then started working as self-employed. Women were more likely than men (18 percent versus 13 percent) to have reduced their hours leading up to retirement and were less likely than men to work after retirement, either full time (4 percent versus 9 percent), part time (11 percent versus 17 percent), or for themselves (6 percent versus 11 percent).

When it came to expenses, nearly three-quarters (74 percent) of those in retirement were drawing Social Security benefits (table 20). Forty-four percent were drawing a traditional defined benefit pension. Nearly a third drew on savings outside a retirement account, 29 percent used savings from an IRA, and 18 percent drew on a defined contribution plan. Nine percent used income from real estate or the sale of real estate to fund expenses in retirement, and 6 percent currently earned wages from a job.

Only 2 percent reported relying on children, grandchildren, or other family members to pay for their expenses. Generally, the sources of funds were similar in retirement for men and women, with no significant differences by gender. The one exception is that men (15 percent) were two-thirds more likely than women (9 percent) to report relying on income from a spouse's job.

About one-third of retirees had retired since 2008. For the vast majority of this group—80 percent—the Great Recession had no effect on their decision to retire. Of the rest of those who retired since 2008, only 4 percent reported that the recession led to them retiring later than they had planned, while 15 percent reported that they had actually retired earlier than planned due to the recession.

Health Insurance Coverage and Health-Care Expenses

To better understand the role that health-care costs and health security play in the financial experiences of households, the survey asked several questions about health insurance and expenditures.

Health Insurance Coverage

According to the survey, 84 percent of respondents were covered by some type of health insurance or health coverage plan when the survey was conducted. The question used to assess insurance coverage in the SHED is identical to the one found in the Census Bureau's American Community Survey (ACS). The SHED finds that approximately 80 percent of people ages 18 to 64, and more than 99 percent of people over age 65, reported some form of health insurance at the time of the survey in September of 2013. (For comparison, estimates of insurance coverage rates for the same groups based on the 2012 ACS data were 79 percent and 99 percent, respectively.)[12]

Health insurance coverage is positively correlated with both income and age. Approximately 76 percent of respondents under the age of 29 had insurance, compared with 79 percent of those ages 30 to 44 and 84 percent of those ages 45 to 64 (table 21). Similarly, among individuals under the age of 65, approximately 69 percent of those who earn less than $25,000 a year had some insurance, compared with 88 percent of those making between $50,000 and $75,000 per year and 96 percent of those making $100,000 or more (table 22).

Coping with Health-Care Costs

Despite the high rate of insurance coverage, out-ofpocket costs were a concern for many respondents. When asked if they could afford to cover the cost of a major out-of-pocket medical expense, 43 percent of all respondents said that it was not likely that they could afford to pay, while 34 percent indicated that it was somewhat likely that they could afford to pay. Only 21 percent of respondents indicated that it was very likely they could afford to pay for a major out-of-pocket medical expense. In fact, almost a quarter of respondents experienced what they described as a major unexpected medical expense that they had to pay out of pocket in the prior 12 months.

This inability to pay factored into individual healthcare decisions, as many respondents reported that they went without some type of care because they were unable to afford it. One quarter of respondents went without dental care in the prior 12 months because they could not afford it, 18 percent went without a doctor visit, 15 percent went without prescription medicine, 11 percent went without a visit to a specialist, and 10 percent went without follow-up care. Overall, 34 percent of respondents reported going without at least one of these types of care because they could not afford it. Not surprisingly, the frequency of foregoing some type of health care was higher among individuals without health insurance. Among those respondents who were uninsured, 53 percent reported that they had gone without some form of medical treatment in the preceding 12 months. In comparison, 30 percent of respondents who had health insurance reported going without some form of medical treatment in the same period.

Table 21. Health insurance coverage (by age) Percent, except as noted

Age categories	Insured	Uninsured
18–29	75.8	24.2
30–44	79.4	20.6
45–64	84.0	16.0
65+	99.6	0.4
Overall	83.8	16.2
Total number of respondents		**4,134**

Table 22. Health insurance coverage (by income among those under age 65) Percent, except as noted

Income categories	Insured	Uninsured
Less than $25,000	69.2	30.8
$25,000–$49,999	76.2	23.8
$50,000–$74,999	87.7	12.3
$75,000–$99,999	94.6	5.4
$100,000 and greater	95.8	4.2
Overall	81.5	18.6
Total number of respondents		**3,102**

Note: Among those who reported their income.

Health-Care Costs and Financial Well-Being

Recognizing that health insurance is just one component of payments for medical care, the survey also allows for a look at the link between medical care and personal savings. Of the people who avoided medical treatment because of the cost, only 16 percent reported having an emergency fund or rainy day fund capable of covering three months of expenses. For people who did not avoid any medical treatment, approximately 52 percent had a rainy day fund. Similarly, 34 percent of people who avoided treatment because of the cost also reported that they regularly save part of their income, compared with 60 percent of the respondents who did not avoid medical treatment.

The survey also indicates that there is a relationship between health-care decisions and some forms of consumer credit. For instance, 44 percent of individuals with student loans reported avoiding medical treatment because they could not afford it, compared with 30 percent of people without student loans. Of people with credit cards, 40 percent of those who said they did not pay their full balance each month also had avoided medical treatment; this compares with 19 percent of people who paid their entire credit card balance and also avoided treatment.[13]

CONCLUSION

The results of this survey tell a complex story of how households in the United States are faring several years after the Great Recession.

In general, it appears that the majority of the population is making progress in recovering from any effects the financial crisis had on their personal finances and household's financial well-being. Most people reported that they are living comfortably or doing okay, and the vast majority expected stable or growing incomes. Additionally, reflecting improvements in the housing market, a plurality of homeowners expect that home prices in their community will rise over the next year.

However, despite these overall reasons for optimism about the economic conditions of U.S. households, the findings in this survey highlight that economic challenges remain for a significant portion of the population. A slight majority of respondents—55 percent—reported saving money in the preceding year. Many report having little financial cushion. A minority of respondents reported having a rainy day fund, and only 56 percent said they could find any way to cover expenses were they to lose their main source of income for three months. Just over one-third reported that they are worse off financially than they were five years ago.

Almost half of respondents reported having given little or no thought to retirement savings, and of those who have, many either do not plan to retire, expect to keep working into retirement to pay for expenses, or do not know how they will pay for their retirement. Nearly a third had no retirement savings whatsoever. These challenges associated with retirement planning were exacerbated by the recession, which resulted in many respondents delaying their planned retirement.

The survey reveals other tensions in households' financial experiences. One-third of those who had applied for credit in the preceding year had been turned down or received less credit than they applied for, and nearly a fifth of respondents put off applying at all because they thought they would be turned down. These experiences and expectations vary by race/ethnicity, with blacks and Hispanics expressing less success and less optimism for success in applying for credit relative to whites. However, this relationship is complex. These differences are at least partially explained once other factors that also vary by race, such as income and education, are included in the analysis.

Furthermore, investment in education—frequently seen as a smart expenditure that pays off over time— may be viewed in varying ways when financed through debt. Nearly one-fourth of respondents reported having some debt related to either their own education or that of someone else. Nearly half reported having to cut back on other spending to service the debt, and 16 percent were behind on their payments or in default. While investment in education is generally rewarded with higher lifetime earnings, respondents with such debt are mixed in their assessment of whether their investment will pay off, with quite a bit of variation by major, type of institution attended, and successful completion of their program of study. Of those who took on debt to help finance their education, respondents who attended public postsecondary institutions were more likely than respondents who attended other institutions to report that the financial benefits outweigh the financial costs they incurred.

Health-care costs were also a source of concern for some respondents. One-third of respondents said that they had foregone some form of medical treatment in the preceding year due to the treatment's expected cost. Not surprisingly, the decision not to seek treatment was more common for those without savings, those indicating that they were struggling with their finances, or those without insurance.

Overall, U.S. households seem to be generally stable, but there is substantial variation across respondents along many indicators of economic well-being. More than five years after the start of the Great Recession, a small, but significant, core of respondents continues to experience economic hardship on multiple dimensions. Moreover, a sizable fraction of respondents appear to be financially vulnerable to unexpected events such as a serious illness, unexpected expense, or job loss.

APPENDIX 1. TECHNICAL APPENDIX ON SURVEY METHODOLOGY

The SHED was designed by Board staff and administered by GfK, an online consumer research company, on behalf of the Board. In order to create a nationally representative probability-based sample, GfK's KnowledgePanel® selected respondents based on both random digit dialing and address-based sampling (ABS). Since 2009 new respondents have been recruited using ABS. To recruit respondents, GfK sends out mailings to a random selection of residential postal addresses. Out of 100 mailings, approximately 14 households contact GfK and express an interest in joining the panel. Of those who contact GfK, three-quarters complete the process and become members of the panel.[14] If the person contacted is interested in participating but does not have a computer or Internet access, GfK provides him or her with a laptop and Internet. Panel respondents are continuously lost to attrition and added to replenish the panel, so the recruitment rate and enrollment rate may vary over time.

For this survey, a total of 6,912 e-mail solicitations to participate in the survey were sent out to a random selection of KnowledgePanel respondents on September 17, 2013, and data collection was terminated on October 4, 2013, with 4,134 surveys fully completed (a completion rate of 59.8 percent) (table 1 of main text). To enhance the completion rate, GfK sent e-mail reminders to non-responders on days three and six of the field period. Respondents were also offered a $10 incentive for completion of the survey. The recruitment rate for this study, reported by GfK, was 13.7 percent and the profile rate was 66.0 percent, for a cumulative response rate of 5.4 percent.

As with any survey method, probability-based Internet panel surveys are subject to potential survey error, such as non-coverage and non-response due to the panel recruitment methods and due to panel attrition. In order to address these potential sources of error, a post-stratification adjustment is applied based on demographic distributions from the most recent (August 2013) data from the Current Population Survey (CPS). The variables used include gender, age, race/ethnicity, education, census region, residence in a metropolitan area, and access to the Internet. The Panel Demographic Post-Stratification weight is applied prior to a probability proportional to size (PPS) selection of a study sample from KnowledgePanel. This weight is designed for sample selection purposes.

Once the sample has been selected and fielded, and all the study data are collected and made final, a post-stratification process is used to adjust for any survey non-response, as well as any non-coverage or under- and over-sampling resulting from the study-specific sample design. Demographic and geographic distributions for the non-institutionalized, civilian population ages 18 and over from the most recent CPS are used as benchmarks in this adjustment.

Comparable distributions are calculated by using all completed cases from the field data. Using the base weight as the starting weight, this procedure adjusts the sample data back to the selected benchmark proportions. Through an iterative convergence process, the weighted sample data are optimally fitted to the marginal distributions.

After this final post-stratification adjustment, the distribution of the calculated weights are examined to identify and, if necessary, trim outliers at the extreme upper and lower tails of the weight distribution. The post-stratified and trimmed weights are then scaled to the sum of the total sample size of all eligible respondents.

There are several reasons that a probability-based Internet panel was selected as the method for this survey rather than an alternative survey method. The first reason is that these types of Internet surveys have been found to be representative of the population.[15] The second reason is that the ABS Internet panel allows the same respondents to be re-interviewed in subsequent surveys with relative ease, as they remain in the panel for several years.

The third reason is that Internet panel surveys have numerous existing data points on respondents from previously administered surveys, including detailed demographic and economic information. This allows for the inclusion of additional information on respondents without increasing respondent burden. Lastly, collecting data through an ABS Internet panel survey is cost effective, and can be done relatively quickly.

APPENDIX 2. SURVEY OF HOUSEHOLD ECONOMICS AND DECISIONMAKING—QUESTIONNAIRE

Below is a reproduction of the survey instrument in its entirety. The bracketed text are programming instructions that (1) indicate whether or not a question is single choice [SP] or multiple choice [MP] and (2) represent any skip pattern used to reach that question and which questions should be grouped together on a page. The respondents only saw the questions and response options; they did not see the program code.

[DISPLAY]

The Federal Reserve Board is interested in learning more about the financial wellbeing and economic perceptions of the American people. This survey covers a broad range of topics related to household finances, financial decisionmaking, and economic conditions. The data collected in this survey will be used for research, analysis, and policymaking on consumer finances and household financial stability. We appreciate your participation in this survey. All respondents who complete this survey will be provided with the equivalent of $10 through the GfK rewards system.

First, tell us a little about yourself.

[SP]

[PROMPT]

D0. Which one of the following best describes your current circumstances?

1. Married
2. Living with significant other/partner
3. Separated or divorced
4. Widowed
5. Single, never married

[SP]
[PROMPT]
D1. Which one of the following BEST describes your living arrangement?

1. Living alone
2. Living with your immediate family (i.e., spouse/partner and/or dependent children, or parents if never married)
3. Living with your adult children
4. Living with your (or your spouse/partner's) extended family (e.g., parents, siblings, cousins)
5. Living with roommate(s)

CREATE DOV [LIVARR] TO BE USED FOR L1 IN THE LIVING ARRANGEMENTS SECTION:

IF D1 = 2 LIVARR = "immediate family"
IF D1 = 3 LIVARR = "adult children"
IF D1 = 4 LIVARR = "extended family"
IF D1 = 5 LIVARR = "roommate(s)" [SP]

[PROMPT]
D2. We are interested in your present job status. Which one of the following BEST describes your current employment situation?

1. Employed now
2. Temporarily laid off
3. Not employed, but looking for a job
4. Not employed and not looking for a job
5. Homemaker
6. Student
7. Disabled
8. Retired

[SP][IF D2 = 1]

D3. Thinking of your main job, do you:

1. Work full time for someone else
2. Work part time for someone else
3. Work for yourself (self-employed)
4. Work in a partnership (e.g., partner in law firm, medical practice)
5. Work as a consultant/contractor

[SP][IF D2 = 6]

D4a. Besides being a student, do you also have a paid job?

1. Yes, I work full time
2. Yes, I work part time
3. No

[SP][IF D2 = 8]

D4b. Besides being retired, do you also have a paid job?

1. Yes, I work full time
2. Yes, I work part time
3. No

[SP][IF D3 = 3]

D4c. Besides being self-employed, do you also have another paid job?

1. Yes, I have another full-time job
2. Yes, I have another part-time job
3. No

[SP][IF D0 = 1 OR 2]

D5. Which one of the following BEST describes your spouse/partner's current employment status?

1. Employed full time
2. Employed part time
3. Not employed, but looking for a job
4. Not employed and not looking for a job
5. Homemaker
6. Student

7. Disabled
8. Retired

Screener/Incidence Questions

[SP][IF D0 = 1 OR 2]

S1A. Do you and/or your spouse/partner currently have a checking, savings, or money market account?

1. Yes
0. No

[SP][IF D0=3-5 or REFUSED]

S1B. Do you currently have a checking, savings, or money market account?

1. Yes
0. No

[SP]

S2. Which one of the following best describes your housing arrangement?

1. I (and/or my spouse/partner) own my home
2. I (and/or my spouse/partner) pay rent
3. I (and/or my spouse/partner) don't own my home or pay rent

[IF S2 = 2 OR 3] [SP]

S3. Have you (and/or your spouse/partner) owned a home in the past 12 months?

1. Yes
0. No

[IF (S2 = 1) AND (D0 = 1 OR 2)]

[SP]

[NOTE: MAKE DEFINITIONS OF HOME EQUITY LOAN AND HOME EQUITY LINE OF CREDIT AVAILABLE TO RESPONDENT IF NEEDED]

[program instruction]

[SHOW THIS DEFINITION IN A POP-UP IF HOME EQUITY LOAN IS CLICKED IN S4]

HEL home equity loan. This is a loan where you borrow a set dollar amount upfront, and pay it back with regular monthly payments. You cannot re-borrow money using this loan even after you have paid some money back.

[SHOW THIS DEFINITION IN A POP-UP IF HOME EQUITY LINE OF CREDIT IS CLICKED IN S5]

HELOC - home equity line of credit. You receive a line of credit for up to a given credit limit (for example, up to $20,000) and can draw on it and make payments on only what you have borrowed. You generally can re-borrow money over time as you pay the money back. You are typically given checks or a bank card to access a HELOC.

S4. Do you (and/or your spouse/partner/significant other) currently have a mortgage on your home? (Do not include home equity lines of credit **[provide pop-up of definition]**)

1. Yes
0. No

IF S4 = 1] [SP]

S5. Do you (and/or your spouse/partner/significant other) currently have a home equity loan **[provide pop-up of definition (using definition laid out from S4)]** or home equity line of credit **[provide pop-up of definition (using definition laid out from S4)]** in addition to your first mortgage?

1. Yes
0. No
8. Don't know

[IF (S2=1) and (D0=3-5 or refused)]

[SP]

S4A. Do you currently have a mortgage on your home? (Do not include home equity lines of credit **[provide pop-up of definition (using definition laid out from S4)]**)

1. Yes
0. No

[IF S4A = 1]

[SP]

S5A. Do you (and/or your spouse/partner/significant other) currently have a home equity loan **[provide pop-up of definition (using definition laid out from S4)]** or home equity line of credit **[provide pop-up of definition (using definition laid out from S4)]** in addition to your first mortgage?

1. Yes
0. No
8. Don't know

[GRID; SP ACROSS]

S7. Do you currently owe any money or have any loans that you used to pay for the education of any of the categories of people below? Please include any loans on which you are the co-signer. If you do not have that particular relationship (e.g., grandchild) please select "Does not apply."

Across:

1. Yes
0. No
999. Does not apply

Down:

a. Your own education
b. Spouse/partner's education
c. Child's education
d. Grandchild's education

IF S7a "Your own education" = 1 "Yes," SET SDEBT1 = 1, ELSE IF S7a "Your own education" = 0 "No," SET SDEBT1 = 0.

IF S7b "Spouse/Partner's education" = 1 "Yes," SET SDEBT2 = 1, ELSE IF S7b "Spouse/Partner's education" = 0 "No," SET SDEBT2 = 0.

IF S7c "Child education" = 1 "Yes," SET SDEBT3 = 1, ELSE IF S7c "Child education" = 0 "No," SET SDEBT3 = 0.

IF S7d "Grandchild education" = 1 "Yes," SET SDEBT4 = 1, ELSE IF S7d

"Grandchild education" = 0 "No," SET SDEBT4 = 0.

[NUMBER BOX]

S11. How many credit cards do you have? **[number box; range 0-25]**

[SP]

S12. In the last 12 months, have you applied for any credit (such as a credit card, mortgage, or other loan)?

1. Yes
0. No

[IF D2 = 8 AND D4b = 3]

[ALLOW RESPONDENT TO EITHER TYPE ANSWER IN NUMBER BOX OR CHECK DON'T KNOW, PROMPT WITH THE FOLLOWING IF BOTH: Please enter an answer in the number box OR check Not sure.]

S13A. At what age did you retire fully, meaning completely stop working?

[Num box 25-99]

999 Not Sure **[SP]**

[IF (D2=1-7 OR REFUSED) or (D4b=1-2)]

[SP]

S13B. In which of the following age ranges do you expect to retire fully, meaning completely stop working for pay?

1. Under 55
2. 56 to 60
3. 61 to 64
4. 65 to 68
5. 69 to 72
6. Over 72
7. Will never stop working
9. Not sure

[GRID; SP ACROSS]

S14. In the past 12 months, Down:

a. Did you spend any money on state lotteries, for example buying Mega Millions, Powerball, or scratch tickets?
b. Did you participate in other types of gambling for money, such as at horse tracks, card rooms, bingo parlors, or casinos?

Across:

1. Yes
0. No

[SP]

S15. Do you own any stock in publicly traded companies directly (i.e., not through a mutual fund or exchange traded fund (ETF))? Please include any stock held in a 401(k) or other pension plan.

1. Yes
0. No
8. Don't know

Rent Section

[ONLY ASK R1 TO R3 IF S2 = 2]
[MP]
[RANDOMIZE 1-7]

R1. Please select all the reason below for why you rent your home rather than own your home?

1. It's cheaper to rent than own a home
2. It's more convenient to rent (for example you can move easily)
3. I plan on moving in the near future
4. I can't qualify for a mortgage to buy a home
5. I can't afford the down payment to buy a home
6. I simply prefer to rent
7. I'm currently looking to buy a home
8. Other (Please specify):**[txt]_____**

[SP]

R2. Over the past 12 months, have you had to cut back on any spending so that you could make your monthly rent payment, and if so, by how much?

0. No
1. Yes, had to cut back a little
2. Yes, had to cut back some
3. Yes, had to cut back a lot

[NUMBER BOX WITH SP]

[ALLOW RESPONDENT TO EITHER TYPE ANSWER IN NUMBER BOX OR CHECK DON'T KNOW, PROMPT WITH THE

FOLLOWING IF BOTH: Please enter an answer in the number box OR check Don't know.]

R3a. About how much do you pay for rent each month?

$ __**[Num box 0-99999]**

888888. Don't know **[SP]**

Own Section

[ONLY ASK H0 – H6 IF S2 = 1]

[NUMBER BOX]

H0. In what year did you buy your current home?

[Num box 1900-2013]

[IF H0 < 2009]

[SP]

H1. Compared to five years ago (since 2008), do you think the value of your home today is higher, lower, or stayed the same?

3. Higher value
2. Value has stayed the same
1. Lower value
8. Don't Know

[SP]

H4. In the next 12 months, how much, if at all, do you think that home prices in your neighborhood will change?

5. Go up by more than 5 percent
4. Go up by 5 percent or less
3. Stay about the same
2. Go down by 5 percent or less
1. Go down by more than 5 percent
8. Don't know

[SP]

H5. Thinking about the past 12 months, did you want to sell your home, but did not or could not?

1. Yes, I put it on the market, but could not sell it
2. Yes, I wanted to sell, but did not put it on the market
3. No, I did not want to sell
4. No, I was able to sell my home, or it's currently on the market

[SP][IF H5 = 1 OR 2]

H6. Was the current market value an important reason for why you did not sell your home?

1. Yes
0. No

Living Arrangement Section

[ONLY ASK L1 – L4 IF (S2 = 2 OR 3) AND (D1 = 3, 4, OR 5)] [IF D0=3-5 or refused]

[SP]

L1. Do you currently live with your [INSERT LIVARR] so that you can save money?

1. Yes
0. No

[IF D0=3-5 or refused]

[SP]

L2. Would you live on your own if you could afford it?

1. Yes
0. No

[IF D0=1 OR 2]

[SP]

L1A. Do you and your family currently live with your [INSERT LIVARR] so that you can save money?

1. Yes
0. No

[IF D0=1 OR 2]

[SP]

L2A. Would you and your family live on your own if you could afford it?

1. Yes
0. No

[DISPLAY IF (S2 = 2 OR 3) AND (D1 = 3, 4, OR 5)][SHOW ON SAME PAGE AS L3]

You previously mentioned that you live with someone other than your immediate family (spouse/partner and dependent children).

[SP, IF (S2 = 2 OR 3) AND (D1 = 3, 4, OR 5)]

L3. Are you (and your family) planning to live on your own in the next 12 months?

4. Definitely yes

3. Probably yes
2. Probably no
1. Definitely no

Credit Application Section

[ASK EVERYONE]
[IF D0= 1 OR 2]
[GRID; SP ACROSS]
[SHOW THIS TEXT INSTEAD OF DEFAULT INSTRUCTIONS: Please answer yes or no to each option]

A1A. In the past 12 months, please tell us if **[IF S12=1 OR REFUSED, INSERT:** each of] the following has or has not happened to you or your spouse/partner: (Please answer yes or no to each option)

PROGRAMMING NOTE: CODE "Yes" AS 1, "No" AS 0, AND REFUSED AS -1.

	1 Yes	0 No
a. **[SHOW IF S12=1 "YES" OR REFUSED]** You/spouse/partner were turned down for credit		
b. **[SHOW IF S12=1 "YES" OR REFUSED]** You/spouse/partner were not given as much credit as you applied for		
c. You/spouse/partner put off applying for credit because you thought you might be turned down		

[IF D0 = 3, 4, OR 5 or refused]
[GRID; SP ACROSS]
[SHOW THIS TEXT INSTEAD OF DEFAULT INSTRUCTIONS: Please answer yes or no to each option]

A1B. In the past 12 months, please tell us if **[IF S12=1 OR REFUSED, INSERT:** each of] the following has or has not happened to you: (Please answer yes or no to each option)

PROGRAMMING NOTE: CODE "Yes" AS 1, "No" AS 0, AND REFUSED AS -1

	1 Yes	0 No
a. **[SHOW IF S12=1 "YES" OR REFUSED]** You were turned down for credit		
b. **[SHOW IF S12=1 "YES" OR REFUSED]** You were not given as much credit as you applied for		
c. You put off applying for credit because you thought you might be turned down		

[SP]

A3. In the past 12 months, have you applied for a mortgage either to refinance an existing mortgage or to buy a home?

1. Yes, to refinance
2. Yes, to buy a home
3. Yes to both refinance AND to buy a home
0. No, have not applied for a mortgage to refinance or buy a home

[SP]

A4. If you were to apply for a mortgage today, how confident are you that your application would be approved?

3. Not confident
2. Somewhat confident
1. Very confident
8. Don't know

[SP][IF A4 = 2 OR 3]

A5. If it became easier to get approved for a mortgage (either to buy a home or refinance) than it is today, how likely is it that you would apply?

4. Very likely
3. Somewhat likely
2. Somewhat unlikely
1. Very unlikely

[SP]

A6. If you were to apply for credit or a loan today (other than a mortgage), how confident are you that your application would be approved?

3. Not confident
2. Somewhat confident
1. Very confident

8. Don't know

[SP][IF S2 = 2 OR 3]

A7. In the past 12 months, have you had a lease application for an apartment or house denied because of your credit history?

1. Yes
0. No

Credit Condition Section

[SP]

C1. If you had to guess, how would you rate your current credit score (such as a FICO score)?

5. Excellent
4. Very good
3. Good
2. Fair
1. Poor
8. Don't know my score or how to rate it

[GRID; SP ACROSS]

[SHOW THIS TEXT INSTEAD OF DEFAULT INSTRUCTIONS: Please answer yes or no to each option]

C2. In the past 12 months, have you:

	1 Yes	0 No
a. Obtained or received a copy of your credit report?		
b. Obtained or received your credit score?		

[SP][IF S11>0]

C3. In the past 12 months, have you always paid your credit card bills in full each month?

1. Yes
0. No

[IF C3=0]

[GRID; SP ACROSS]

[SHOW THIS TEXT INSTEAD OF DEFAULT INSTRUCTIONS: Please answer yes or no to each option]

C4. Also, in the past 12 months, have you ever:

	1 Yes	0 No
a. Carried over a balance on your credit card and been charged interest		
b. Paid only the minimum payment on one or more of your credit card bills		
c. Carried a balance on your credit card at a low-interest rate from a special offer or promotion		
d. Used a credit card for a cash advance		

Student Loans

[ONLY ASK T1 – T8 IF SDEBT1 = 1 OR SDEBT2 = 1 OR SDEBT3 = 1 OR SDEBT4 = 1]

[DISPLAY IF SDEBT1 = 1 OR SDEBT2 = 1 OR SDEBT3 = 1 OR SDEBT4 = 1]

In this section we would like to ask you about your experience borrowing to pay for education.

NOTE: FOR T1 SET VARIABLE NAMES TO BE T1 + COLUMN IDENTIFIER + ROW IDENTIFIER, E.G., T1A1. KEEP ROW IDENTIFIERS TIED TO TYPE OF LOAN (1 = YOUR EDUCATION, 2 = YOUR SPOUSE/PARTNER'S, 3 = CHILD, 4 = GRANDCHILD). SET ALL YES ANSWER = 1 AND ALL NO ANSWER = 0.

[GRID WITH NUMBER BOXES AND CHECK BOXES (next to each check box, put "Yes" [Yes])]

[COLUMN A NUMBER BOXES RANGE: 1-25]

[ONLY SHOW ROWS WHERE S7=1 YES]T1. For each person whose education you've borrowed money for, please tell us how many loans you've taken out and answer Yes or No to each of the four questions for the loans you have.

	Loans	A	B	C	D	E
		Number of loans	Making payment on one or more of these Loans now?	One or more loans are in deferment/ forbearance so do not need to make payments right now?	Behind on payments for one or more of these loans?	One or more of these loans is in collections?
1	For Your Education	RECORD ACTUAL	PROGRAMMINGNOTE:INSERTYes/Noboxes INTOCELLS.CODE"YES"AS1.CODE"NO"AS0.			
2	For Your Spouse's/ Partner's Education	RECORD ACTUAL				
3	For Your Child's Education	RECORD ACTUAL				
4	For Your Grandchild's Education	RECORD ACTUAL				

[GRID WITH NUMBER BOXES]

[RANGE FOR ALL NUMBER BOXES; 0-10000000]

[ONLY SHOW ROWS WHERE S7=1 YES]T1A. Please provide a little more information on the amount owed for each person's education and the monthly payment that you make, if any at this time. If no monthly payment is made, please enter 0 (zero). If you don't know the exact amount an estimate is fine.

Loans	F Total $amount owed	G Total $amount of monthly payment on these loans
1 For Your Education		
2 For Your Spouse's/ Partner's Education		
3 For Your Child's Education		
4 For Your Grandchild's Education		

[Display IF SDEBT1 = 1]

The following questions ask about the education program that you borrowed money to pay for. When we say educational program we mean any type of degree, certificate, or diploma. If you borrowed money to pay for yourself to enroll in more than one educational program, when answering the next five questions please refer to the most recent program for which you acquired a loan.

[IF SDEBT1 = 1]
[SP]

T2. Did you complete the most recent educational program for which you borrowed money?

1. Yes
0. No
2. Still enrolled in the program

[IF T2 = 1] [NUMBER BOX]

T3. In what year did you complete the program that you borrowed the money for?

______**[RANGE: 1900 – 2013]**

[IF SDEBT1 = 1]
[SP]

T4. Overall, how would you say the lifetime financial benefits of your most recent educational program compare to the lifetime financial costs to you of this education?

1. Much larger financial benefits than costs
2. Somewhat larger financial benefits than costs
3. About same financial benefits and costs
4. Somewhat smaller financial benefits than costs

5. Much smaller financial benefits than costs

[IF SDEBT1 = 1]
[TEXT BOX]
T5. What is the name of the school that you borrowed money to attend?

[IF SDEBT1 = 1]
[SP]
T6. Which one of the following broad categories best describes your major at the school you borrowed money to attend?

1. Humanities
2. Social/behavioral sciences
3. Life sciences
4. Physical sciences/math
5. Computer/information sciences
6. Engineering
7. Education
8. Business/management
9. Health
10. Law
11. Vocational/technical training
12. Undeclared
13. Other (Please specify): **[TXT]** ______

[IF SDEBT1 = 1]
[SP]
T7. Still thinking about your most recent educational program, what type of degree or credential did you borrow money for?

1. Certificate or technical training
2. Associate's degree
3. Bachelor's degree
4. Master's degree
5. Professional degree (e.g., MBA, MD, JD)
6. Doctoral degree
7. Other (Please specify):**[txt]**______

[IF T1B1, T1B2, T1B3, OR T1B4=1] [SP]
T8. Over the past 12 months, have you had to cut back on any spending so that you could make your monthly student loan payment?

0. No

1. Yes, had to cut back a little
2. Yes, had to cut back a lot

Health Insurance/Expense Section

[ASK EVERYONE]
[GRID; SP ACROSS]
[SHOW THIS TEXT INSTEAD OF DEFAULT INSTRUCTIONS: Please answer yes or no to each option]

E1. During the past 12 months, was there a time when you needed any of the following, but didn't get it because you couldn't afford it?

PROGRAMMING NOTE: CODE "Yes" AS 1, "No" AS 0, AND REFUSED AS -1.

	1 Yes	0 No
a. Prescription medicine (including taking less medication than prescribed)		
b. To see a doctor		
c. Mental health care or counseling		
d. Dental care (including check-ups or routine cleaning)		
e. To see a specialist (such as an OB/GYN, dermatologist, orthopedic surgeon, etc.)		
f. Follow-up care (e.g., going to physical therapy sessions recommended by a doctor)		

[SP]

E2. During the past 12 months, have you had any unexpected major medical expenses that you had to pay out of pocket (that were not completely paid for by insurance)?

1. Yes
0. No

[SP]

E3. If you were to have a major unexpected medical expense that you had to pay for out of pocket, how likely is it that you that you would be able to pay your medical bills?

3. Very likely

2. Somewhat likely
1. Not likely

[GRID; SP ACROSS]

[SHOW THIS TEXT INSTEAD OF DEFAULT INSTRUCTIONS: Please answer yes or no to each option]

E4. Are you CURRENTLY covered by any of the following types of health insurance or health coverage plans?

PROGRAMMING NOTE: CODE "Yes" AS 1, "No" AS 0, AND REFUSED AS -1.

	1 Yes	0 No
a. Insurance through a current or former employer or union (of yourself or a family member)		
b. Insurance purchased directly from an insurance company (by yourself or a family member)		
c. Medicare, for people 65 or older, or people with certain disabilities		
d. Medicaid, Medical Assistance, or any kind of government-assistance plan for those with low incomes or disability		
e. TRICARE or other military health care		
f. VA (including those who have ever used or enrolled for VA health care)		
g. Indian Health Service		
h. Any other type of health insurance or health coverage plan		

Financial Management and Stability

[ASK EVERYONE]

[GRID; SP ACROSS; RANDOMIZE]

B1. In order to help us to understand your role in the financial activities of your household, please tell us how much responsibility you have for the following financial tasks.

Down:

a. Paying monthly bills (rent or mortgage, utilities, cell phone, etc.)
b. Managing the household's savings and investments

Across:

a. None or almost none
b. Some
c. Shared equally with other household members
d. Most
e. All or almost all

[SP]

B2. Which one of the following best describes how well you are managing financially these days:

4. Living comfortably
3. Doing okay
2. Just getting by
1. Finding it difficult to get by

[SP]

B3. Compared to five years ago (2008), would you say that you (and your family living with you) are better off, the same, or worse off financially?

5. Much better off
4. Somewhat better off
3. About the same
2. Somewhat worse
1. Much worse

Retirement Planning

[ASK EVERYONE]

IF D2 NOT = 8, ASK K1 THROUGH K8. IF D2 = 8, ASK K9 THROUGH K13.

[DISPLAY]

In this section we would like to ask you about your plans for retiring from the workforce and paying for your expenses in retirement.

[SP][ASK IF D2 = 1-7 or Refused]

K0. How much thought have you given to the financial planning for your retirement?

0. None at all
1. A little
2. Some
3. A fair amount

4. A lot

[SP][IF K0 = 2, 3 OR 4]

K1. Which one of the following best describes your plan for retirement?

a. I do not plan to retire **[EXCLUSIVE]**
b. Work fewer hours as I get close to retirement
c. Retire from my current career, but then find a different full-time job
d. Retire from my current career, but then find a different part-time job
e. Retire from my current career, but then work for myself
f. Work full time until I retire, then stop working altogether g.Keep working as long as possible
h. Other (Please specify): **[TXT] ____**

[MP; RANDOMIZE B-G]

[ASK IF D2 = 1-7 or Refused]

K2. Please tell us what type(s) of retirement savings or pension you (or your spouse/partner) have.

a. No retirement savings or pension **[EXCLUSIVE]**
b. Social Security benefits
c. 401(k), 403(b), Thrift or other defined contribution pension plan through an employer
d. Defined benefit pension through an employer (i.e., pension based on a formula, your earnings, and years of service)
e. Individual Retirement Account (IRA)
f. Savings outside a retirement account (e.g., a brokerage account, savings account)
g. Real estate or land
h. Other (Please specify):**[txt]_____**

[ASK IF (K1a IS NOT SELECTED) AND (D2 = 1-7 or Refused)]

[MP; RANDOMZE A I]

K3. How are you (and your spouse/partner) planning to pay for your expenses in retirement? Please select all that apply.

a. Social Security Old-Age benefits
b. I will continue working
c. Spouse/partner will continue working
d. Defined benefit pension from work (i.e., pension based on a formula, your earnings, and years of service)
e. 401(k), 403(b), Thrift or other defined contribution pension plan from work
f. Individual Retirement Account (IRA)

g. Savings outside a retirement account (e.g., a brokerage account, savings account)
h. Income from real estate or the sale of real estate
i. Income from a business or the sale of a business
j. Rely on children, grandchildren, or other family
k. I don't know **[SP]**
l. Other (Please specify):**[txt]**

[ASK IF (K0 = 2, 3 OR 4) AND (D2 = 1-7 or Refused)]
[SP]

K4. Compared to your retirement plans before 2008, would you say that you now plan to retire earlier, at the same age, later than what you had planned to do at that time?

1. Plan to retire earlier
2. Plan to retire at the same age
3. Plan to retire later
8. Didn't think about retirement prior to 2008

[DISPLAY K5 AND K6 ON THE SAME SCREEN]
[ASK IF (K2a IS NOT SELECTED) AND (D2 = 1-7 or Refused)]
[SP]

K5. In the past 12 months, have you borrowed money from any of your retirement savings accounts?

1. Yes
0. No

[ASK IF (K2a IS NOT SELECTED) AND (D2 = 1-7 or Refused)]
[SP]

K6. In the past 12 months, have you cashed out any of your retirement savings (permanently withdrawn the money)?

1. Yes
0. No

[IF D2 = 1-7 or Refused]
[NUMBER BOX]

K7. On a scale from 0 to 10, where 0 is no chance and 10 is absolutely certain, and you can use any number in between, what are the chances that you will live to at least age 75?

[Num box, 0-10] ____

[IF D2 = 1-7 or Refused] [NUMBER BOX]

K8. On a scale from 0 to 10, where 0 is no chance and 10 is absolutely certain, and you can use any number in between, what are the chances that you will live to at least age 85?

[Num box, 0-10] ____
[ASK IF D2 = 8]
[SHOW THIS TEXT INSTEAD OF DEFAULT INSTRUCTIONS: Please answer yes or no to each option]

K9. Thinking about your transition to retirement, please tell us if any of the following happened to you: (Please answer Yes or No to each option)

PROGRAMMING NOTE: CODE "Yes" AS 1, "No" AS 0, AND REFUSED AS -1.

	1 Yes	0 No
a. Worked fewer hours as I got close to retirement		
b. Retired from my previous career, but then found a different full-time job		
c. Retired from my previous career, but then found a different part-time job		
d. Retired from my previous career, but then started working as self-employed		
e. Worked full time until I retired, then stopped working altogether		

[ASK IF D2 = 8]
[MP; RANDOMIZE A – I]

K10. Are you (and your spouse/partner) using any of these to pay for your expenses in retirement? Please select all that apply.

a. Social Security Old-Age benefits
b. I have a job
c. My spouse/partner has a job
d. Defined benefit pension from work (i.e., pension based on a formula, your earnings, and years of service)
e. 401(k), 403(b), Thrift or other defined contribution pension plan from work
f. Individual Retirement Account (IRA)
g. Savings outside a retirement account (e.g., a brokerage account, savings account)
h. Income from real estate or the sale of real estate i. Income from a business or the sale of a business
j. Relying on children, grandchildren, or other family
k. Other (Please specify):**[txt]_____**

[SP][IF D2 = 8 AND (xyear + S13A) >= 2008]

K11. Did the recent recession affect your decision to retire?

1. Yes, retired earlier than planned
2. Yes, retired later than planned
0. No

[IF D2 = 8 AND XYEAR > 1938]

K12. On a scale from 0 to 10, where 0 is no chance and 10 is absolutely certain, and you can use any number in between, what are the chances that you will live to at least age 75?

[Num box, 0-10] ___

[IF D2 = 8 AND XYEAR > 1928, ASK:]

K13. On a scale from 0 to 10, where 0 is no chance and 10 is absolutely certain, and you can use any number in between, what are the chances that you will live to at least age 85?

[Num box, 0-10] ___

Recession Recovery Section

[ASK EVERYONE]

[DISPLAY]

The questions in this section are about how the recent recession that began in 2008 affected you and your household's finances.

[SP]

X1. Since 2008, have you or your family living with you experienced any significant major life change or financial hardship such as a job loss, drop in income, health emergency, divorce, or loss of your home?

1. Yes
0. No

[MP; RANDOMIZE A J]

[IF X1 = 1]

X2. Which of the following did you or your family living with you experience since

2008?

PROGRAMMING NOTE: CODE SELECTED ITEMS AS 1 AND NONSELECTED ITEMS AS 0.

a. I lost a job
b. I had my work hours and/or pay reduced
c. My spouse/partner lost a job

d. My spouse/partner had their work hours and/or pay reduced
e. Received a foreclosure notice
f. A business I owned had financial difficulty
g. Had a health emergency
h. Divorce
i. Had a baby
j. Death of primary breadwinner
k. Other (Please specify):**[TXT]** ___

[SP]

X3. Did you delay any major expenses or purchases because of the recession that began in 2008, such as buying a house, a car, appliance, or going on vacation?

1. Yes
0. No

[MP; RANDOMIZE A-D] [IF X3=1]

X4. What major purchase(s) did you delay?

PROGRAMMING NOTE: CODE SELECTED ITEMS AS 1 AND NONSELECTED ITEMS AS 0.

a. Buying a home
b. Buying a car
c. Buying a major appliance
d. Going on vacation
e. Home improvements
f. Other (Please specify): **[TXT]** ___

[SP]

X5. Did you delay any major life decisions because of the recession that began in 2008, such as marriage, having a child, retirement, buying a home, or moving?

1. Yes
0. No

[MP; RANDOMIZE A-E] [IF X5 = 1]

X6. What major life decision(s) did you delay?

PROGRAMMING NOTE: CODE SELECTED ITEMS AS 1 AND NONSELECTED ITEMS AS 0.

a. Marriage
b. Retirement
c. Having a child
d. Buying a home
e. Moving to a new city or state

f. Changing jobs
g. Other (Please specify): **[TXT]** ____________________

[SP]

X7. Before 2008, did you or your household have any savings, including stocks, money in a savings account, or pensions?

1. Yes
0. No
8. Don't know

[SP]
[IF X7 = 1]

X8. Since 2008, have you or your household had to use up some, nearly all, or all of your savings to pay for bills and expenses?

1. Yes, some
2. Yes, nearly all
3. Yes, all
0. No

[SP]

X9. Since 2008, have you or your household received any financial assistance from your family or a friend?

1. Yes
0. No

[SP]

X10. Since 2008, have you or your household provided any financial assistance to a friend or family member?

1. Yes
0. No

[Textbox, 150 characters]

X11. In a sentence or two please describe the main financial challenges or concerns facing you or your family? If none please click the "None" box.

999 None **[SP]**

Labor Market and Skills

[ASK Y1 – Y4 IF D2 = 1-6 OR REFUSED]
[DISPLAY IF D2 = 1-6 OR REFUSED]

The questions in this section are about your work experience, job skills, and job readiness.

[SP]

Y1. Thinking about your current education and work experience, how confident are you that you have the skills necessary to get the kinds of jobs you want now?

1. Very confident
2. Somewhat confident
3. Not confident
4. I am not currently in the workforce and I am not looking for a job
8. Don't know

[SP]

Y2. Thinking about the types of jobs you believe will be available in ten years, how confident are you that you have the skills necessary to get the kinds of jobs you want?

1. Very confident
2. Somewhat confident
3. Not confident
4. I do not expect to be working ten years from now
8. Don't know

[IF Y1 = 3 AND Y2 = 1, 2, OR 8 OR REFUSED, ASK Y3] [IF Y1 = 1, 2, OR 8 OR REFUSED AND Y2 = 3, ASK Y4]

[IF Y1 = 3 AND Y2 = 3, RANDOMLY ASSIGN TO Y3 OR Y4 (DO NOT ASK BOTH) AND RECORD IN DOV_Y3Y4]

[MP]

Y3. You expressed some lack of confidence in your skills for the kinds of jobs that you might want today. Which of these statements, if any, do you agree with?

1. I need more education or another degree
2. I need more job training
3. My skills are out of date because I haven't been using them
4. The job market is changing faster than I can keep up with
5. The kind of job I'm qualified for is not available

[MP]

Y4. You expressed some lack of confidence in your skills for the kinds of jobs that you will want in ten years. Which of these statements, if any, do you agree with?

1. I will need more education or another degree to be competitive
2. I will need more job training to be competitive

3 My skills will be out of date in ten years
4. The job market will change faster than I can keep up with
5. The kind of job I'm qualified for may not be available in ten years

Income and Consumption Section

[ASK EVERYONE]
[SP]

I1. In 2012, would you say that your household's total spending was more than your income, that it was about the same as your income, or that you spent less than your income?

3. Spending was more than income
2. Spending was same as income
1. Spending was less than income

[NUMBER BOX]

I2. In 2012, about how much of your income did your household set aside as savings as a percent of your total gross household income (before taxes and deductions)?

Please include all types of savings, even those through a pension or 401(k) at work. If you did not save any money in 2012 please enter zero in the box below.

_______% [NUM-BOX 0 TO 100]

[MP; RANDOMIZE A J]

[IF I2 > 0]

I3. Which of the following categories, if any, are you saving money for? PROGRAMMING NOTE: CODE SELECTED ITEMS AS 1 AND NON-SELECTED ITEMS AS 0.

a. Education (yours or someone else's)
b. Retirement
c. Your children
d. Major appliance, car, or other big purchase (excluding a home)
e. Home purchase
f. Pay off debts
g. Unexpected expenses
i. Taxes
h. Just to save
j. To leave behind some inheritance or charitable donation
k. Other (Please specify):**[txt]_____**

[NUMBER BOX]

I4. How much was the total income your household received in 2012 from all sources, before taxes and other deductions were made?

$**__________[NUM box 0-9999999]**

999999999999 REFUSED

[SP][IF I4 = REFUSED]

I4A. Which of the following categories best describes your total household income from all sources, before taxes and deductions, in 2012?

1. $0 to $4,999
2. $5,000 to $14,999
3. $15,000 to $24,999
4. $25,000 to $49,999
5. $50,000 to $74,999
6. $75,000 to $99,999
7. $100,000 to $149,999
8. $150,000 to $199,999
9. $200,000 to $249,000
10. $250,000 or higher

[SP]

I5. Was your total household income in 2012 higher or lower compared to what you would expect in a normal year, or was it normal?

3. High
1. Low
2. Normal

[IF I5 = 3 or 1]

I6. What would you say your total household income is in a normal year?

$**_______**[NUM BOX 0-9999999]

999999999999 REFUSED

[SP][IF I5 = (3 or 1) AND (I6 = REFUSED)]

I6A. Which of the following categories best describes your total household income in a normal year?

1. $0 to $4,999
2. $5,000 to $14,999
3. $15,000 to $24,999
4. $25,000 to $49,999
5. $50,000 to $74,999
6. $75,000 to $99,999
7. $100,000 to $149,999
8. $150,000 to $199,999

9. $200,000 to $249,000
10. $250,000 or higher

[SP]

I7. During the next 12 months, do you expect your total income to be higher, about the same, or lower than during the past 12 months?

3. Higher
2. About the same
1. Lower

[NUMBER BOXES]

I8. If you received $1,000 in unexpected income today, such as a bonus at work, how much of the $1,000 you would spend, how much you would save, and how much you would use to pay down any debt within one month?

a. Spend: $

b. Save: $______

c. Pay down existing debt: $______ **[Num boxes 0-1000; total must sum to 1000]**

[SP]

I9. Which one of the following best describes how your household's income changes from month to month, if at all?

1. Roughly the same amount each month
2. Roughly the same most months, but some unusually high or low months during the year
3. Often varies quite a bit from one month to the next

[MP; RANDOMIZE; A-F]]

[IF I9 = 2 OR 3]

I10. Please indicate whether each of the following is a reason that your income changes from month to month: (Select all that apply)

PROGRAMMING NOTE: CODE SELECTED ITEMS AS 1 AND NONSELECTED ITEMS AS 0.

a. Bonuses
b. Commissions
c. Seasonal employment
d. Irregular work schedule (i.e., your work hours change from week to week)
e. Periods of unemployment f. Investment Income
g. Other (Please specify:)**[TXT]: __**

Emergency Fund

[RANDOMLY ASSIGN PARTICIPANTS TO E1A OR E1B AND RECORD IN DOV]

[SP]

E1A. If you were to lose your main source of income (e.g., job, government benefits), could you cover your expenses for 3 months by borrowing money, using savings, selling assets, or borrowing from friends/family?

1. Yes
0. No

[SP]

E1B. Have you set aside emergency or rainy day funds that would cover your expenses for 3 months in case of sickness, job loss, economic downturn, or other emergencies?

1. Yes
0. No

[MP]

E3b. Suppose that you have an emergency expense that costs $400. **Based on your current financial situation** how would you pay for this expense? If you would use more than one method to cover this expense please select all that apply.

PROGRAMMING NOTE: CODE SELECTED ITEMS AS 1 AND NONSELECTED ITEMS AS 0.

a. Put it on my credit card and pay it off in full at the next statement
b. Put it on my credit card and pay it off over time
c. With the money currently in my checking/savings account or with cash
d. Using money from a bank loan or line of credit
e. By borrowing from a friend or family member
f. Using a payday loan, deposit advance, or overdraft
g. By selling something
h. I wouldn't be able to pay for the expense right now
i. Other (Please specify):**[txt]** ______

[SP][ASK E4b IF S1a= 1 OR S1b = 1]

E4b. Do you regularly set aside part of any income you receive in some type of savings account?

1. Yes
0. No

Gambling/Risky Behavior Section

[ASK G1G3 IF S14A =1 OR S14B =1 OR S15 = 1]
[SP; RANDOMIZE 1-3]
[IF S14A =1 OR S14B =1]

G1. Which one of these is the main reason that you play lotteries or other types of gambling?

1. For the money or prizes
2. As a pastime or for entertainment
3. As a form of charitable donation
4. Other [Please specify]: ______

[SP]
[IF S14A =1 OR S14B =1]

G2. During the past 12 months, about how much money would you say that you spent on state lotteries and other types of gambling?

1. Less than $100
2. $100 to $249
3. $250 to $499
4. More than $500
8. Don't know

[SP][IF S15 = 1]

G3. In a typical year, about how often do you buy or sell stocks in individual companies, including trades in a retirement account like a 401(k)? Please do not include buying or selling stock mutual funds or Exchange Traded Funds (ETFs).

1. Buy or sell at least once a week
2. Buy or sell at least once a month
3. Buy or sell at least once a quarter
4. Buy or sell at least once a year
5. Buy or sell less than once a year

Demographics/Attitudes

ASK EVERYONE
*** RISK ATTITUDES ****
[SP]

P3. Which one of the following statements comes closest to describing the amount of financial risk that you are willing to take when you save or make investments?

1. Take substantial financial risks expecting to earn substantial returns
2. Take above average financial risks expecting to earn above average returns
3. Take average financial risks expecting to earn average returns
4. Not willing to take any financial risks

[DISPLAY]

The following sequence of questions is used by us to figure out how willing you are personally to take risks. You will be asked to compare two jobs that offer you different potential incomes and then to pick the one that you prefer. This is not a test and there are no 'right' answers.

[SP]

P4. Suppose that you are the only income earner in the family. You have to choose between the following two possible jobs. Which job would you take?

RANDOMLY DISPLAY ONE JOB ON THE LEFT HAND SIDE OF THE SCREEN AND THE OTHER ON THE RIGHT HAND SIDE. PROVIDE RADIAL BUTTONS FOR THE SELECTION OF ONE JOB. **REGARDLESS OF DISPLAYED SIDE, MAINTAIN LABELS OF "FIRST JOB" AND "SECOND JOB" FOR PROGRAMMING LOGIC.** DO NOT DISPLAY "FIRST JOB" OR "SECOND JOB."

FIRST JOB: This job would guarantee your current total family income for life.

SECOND JOB: This job is better paying, but the income is also less certain. There is a 50-50 chance this job would double your total lifetime income and a 50-50 chance that it would cut it by a third.

[SP] [IF P4 = FIRST JOB]

P5. Now which job would you take?

PROVIDE RADIAL BUTTONS FOR THE SELECTION OF ONE JOB. DO NOT DISPLAY "FIRST JOB" OR "SECOND JOB."

MAINTAIN ORDER FROM Q4:

FIRST JOB: This job would guarantee your current total family income for life.

SECOND JOB: This job is better paying, but the income is also less certain. **Suppose the chances were 50-50 that this job would double your lifetime income and 50-50 that it would cut it by 20 percent.**

[SP][IF P4 = SECOND JOB]

P6. Now which job would you take?

PROVIDE RADIAL BUTTONS FOR THE SELECTION OF ONE JOB. DO NOT DISPLAY "FIRST JOB" OR "SECOND JOB."

MAINTAIN ORDER FROM P4:

FIRST JOB: This job would guarantee your current total family income for life.

SECOND JOB: This job is better paying, but the income is also less certain. **Suppose the chances were 50-50 that this job would double your lifetime income, and 50-50 that it would cut it in half.**

[SP][IF P6 = SECOND JOB]

P7. Now which job would you take?

PROVIDE RADIAL BUTTONS FOR THE SELECTION OF ONE JOB. DO NOT DISPLAY "FIRST JOB" OR "SECOND JOB."

MAINTAIN ORDER FROM P4:

FIRST JOB: This job would guarantee your current total family income for life.

SECOND JOB: This job is better paying, but the income is also less certain. **Suppose the chances were 50-50 that this job would double your lifetime income and 50-50 that it would cut it by 75 percent.**

[SP][IF P5 = FIRST JOB]

P8. Now which job would you take?

PROVIDE RADIAL BUTTONS FOR THE SELECTION OF ONE JOB. DO NOT DISPLAY "FIRST JOB" OR "SECOND JOB."

MAINTAIN ORDER FROM P4:

FIRST JOB: This job would guarantee your current total family income for life.

SECOND JOB: This job is better paying, but the income is also less certain. **Suppose the chances were 50-50 that this job would double your lifetime income and 50-50 that it would cut it by 10 percent.**

[INSERT STANDARD CLOSE] (In standard close change wording to "survey" not "topic")

APPENDIX 3. CONSUMER RESPONSES TO SURVEY QUESTIONNAIRE

Not all questions were asked to all respondents.

Table C.1. Which one of the following best describes your current circumstances? Percent, except as noted

Response	Rate
Refused	0.2
Married	50.3
Living with significant other/partner	8.4
Separated or divorced	11.3
Widowed	4.8
Single, never married	25.1
Number of respondents	**4,134**

Table C.2. Which one of the following BEST describes your living arrangement? Percent, except as noted

Response	Rate
Refused	0.2
Living alone	21.9
Living with your immediate family	61.4
Living with your adult children	2.7
Living with your (or your spouse/partner's) extended family	8.9
Living with roommate(s)	4.9
Number of respondents	**4,134**

Table C.3. We are interested in your present job status. Which one of the following BEST describes your current employment situation? Percent, except as noted

Response	Rate
Refused	0.2
Employed now	51.7
Temporarily laid off	0.6
Not employed, but looking for a job	7.7
Not employed and not looking for a job	2.0
Homemaker	5.4
Student	4.4
Disabled	8.5
Retired	19.4
Number of respondents	**4,134**

Table C.4. Thinking of your main job, do you: Percent, except as noted

Response	Rate
Refused	0.4
Work full time for someone else	75.3
Work part time for someone else	16.3
Work for yourself (self-employed)	7.2
Work in a partnership (e.g., partner in law firm, medical practice)	0.3
Work as a consultant/contractor	0.6
Number of respondents	**2,149**

Table C.5. Besides being a student, do you also have a paid job? Percent, except as noted

Response	Rate
Yes, I work full time	4.1
Yes, I work part time	44.6
No	51.3
Number of respondents	**145**

Table C.6. Besides being retired, do you also have a paid job? Percent, except as noted

Response	Rate
Refused	0.9
Yes, I work full time	0.6
Yes, I work part time	9.5
No	89.0
Number of respondents	**971**

Table C.7. Besides being self-employed, do you also have another paid job? Percent, except as noted

Response	Rate
Yes, I have another full-time job	2.5
Yes, I have another part-time job	15.6
No	81.9
Number of respondents	**178**

Table C.8. Which one of the following BEST describes your spouse/ partner's current employment status? Percent, except as noted

Response	Rate
Refused	0.3
Employed full time	56.1
Employed part time	7.7
Not employed, but looking for a job	4.6
Not employed and not looking for a job	1.7
Homemaker	7.1
Student	1.0
Disabled	4.1
Retired	17.3
Number of respondents	**2,617**

Table C.9. Do you or your spouse/partner have a checking, savings, or money market account? Percent, except as noted

Response	Rate
Refused	0.8
No	9.6
Yes	89.7
Number of respondents	**4,134**

Table C.10. Which one of the following best describes your housing arrangement? Percent, except as noted

Response	Rate
Refused	0.9
I (and/or my spouse/partner) own my home	57.9
I (and/or my spouse/partner) pay rent	32.0
I (and/or my spouse/partner) don't own my home or pay rent	9.2
Number of respondents	**4,134**

Table C.11. Have you (and/or your spouse/partner) owned a home in the past 12 months? Percent, except as noted

Response	Rate
Refused	0.3
No	94.2
Yes	5.5
Number of respondents	**1,368**

Table C.12. Do you (and/or your spouse/partner/significant other) currently have a mortgage on your home? Percent, except as noted

Response	Rate
Refused	0.9
No	36.5
Yes	62.6
Number of respondents	**2,732**

Table C.13. Do you (and/or your spouse/partner/significant other) currently have a home equity loan or home equity line of credit in addition to your first mortgage? Percent, except as noted

Response	Rate
Refused	0.3
No	74.5
Yes	20.0
Don't know	5.3
Number of respondents	**1,675**

Table C.14. Do you currently owe any money or have any loans that you used to pay for the education of anyone below? Percent, except as noted

Response	Rate
Your own education	15.8
Spouse/partner's education	7.5
Child's education	5.7
Grandchild's education	0.6
Number of respondents	**4,134**

Table C.15. In the last 12 months, have you applied for any credit? Percent, except as noted

Response	Rate
Refused	1.2
No	67.4
Yes	31.4
Number of respondents	**4,134**

Table C.16. In which of the following age ranges do you expect to retire fully? Percent, except as noted

Response	Rate
Refused	1.2
Under 55	6.0
56 to 60	9.2
Response	**Rate**
61 to 64	13.1
65 to 68	23.5
69 to 72	11.2
Over 72	6.4
Will never stop working	8.6
Not sure	20.9
Number of respondents	**3,275**

**Table C.17. In the past 12 months, did you spend any money on state lotteries?
Percent, except as noted**

Response	Rate
Refused	1.2
No	55.1
Yes	43.7
Number of respondents	**4,134**

Table C.18. In the past 12 months, did you participate in other types of gambling for money?
Percent, except as noted

Response	Rate
Refused	1.1
No	81.5
Yes	17.4
Number of respondents	**4,134**

Table C.19. Do you own any stock in publicly traded companies directly?
Percent, except as noted

Response	Rate
Refused	1.2
No	59.6
Yes	33.0
Don't know	6.2
Number of respondents	**4,134**

Table C.20. Please select all the reasons below for why you rent your home rather than own your home:
Percent, except as noted

Response	Rate
Cheaper to rent than own	22.8
More convenient to rent	24.4
I plan on moving in the near future	20.1
Can't qualify for a mortgage	29.1
Can't afford down payment	45.3
Prefer to rent	19.6
Currently looking to buy a home	9.7
Other	8.9
Refused	1.6
1,051	**1,051**

Table C.21. Over the past 12 months, have you had to cut back on any spending so that you could make your monthly rent payment? Percent, except as noted

Response	Rate
Refused	1.3
No	43.6
Yes, had to cut back a little	23.3
Yes, had to cut back some	15.2
Yes, had to cut back a lot	16.7
Number of respondents	**1,051**

Table C.22. Compared to five years ago (since 2008), do you think the value of your home today is higher, lower, or stayed the same? Percent, except as noted

Response	Rate
Refused	0.8
Lower value	45.2
Value has stayed the same	19.5
Higher value	26.9
Don't Know	7.5
Number of respondents	**2,222**

Table C.23. In the next 12 months, how much, if at all, do you think that home prices in your neighborhood will change? Percent, except as noted

Response	Rate
Refused	0.4
Go down by more than 5 percent	3.4
Go down by 5 percent or less	4.9
Stay about the same	36.8
Go up by 5 percent or less	25.8
Go up by more than 5 percent	13.5
Don't know	15.1
Number of respondents	**2,732**

Table C.24. Thinking about the past 12 months, did you want to sell your home, but did not or could not? Percent, except as noted

Response	Rate
Refused	1.0
Yes, I put it on the market, but could not sell it	1.9
Yes, I wanted to sell, but did not put it on the market	9.1
No, I did not want to sell	85.6
No, I was able to sell my home, or it's currently on the market	2.5
Number of respondents	**2,732**

Table C.25. Was the current market value an important reason for why you did not sell your home? Percent, except as noted

Response	Rate
Refused	0.3
No	27.3
Yes	72.4
Number of respondents	**277**

Table C.26. Do you and/or your spouse/partner live with someone else so you can save money? Percent, except as noted

Response	Rate
Refused	1.4
No	48.0
Yes	50.6
Number of respondents	**327**

Table C.27. Would you live on your own if you could afford it? Percent, except as noted

Response	Rate
Refused	1.6
No	25.2
Yes	73.2
Number of respondents	**327**

**Table C.28. Are you (and your family) planning to live on your own in the next 12 months?
Percent, except as noted**

Response	Rate
Refused	3.2
Definitely no	22.0
Probably no	32.2
Probably yes	19.7
Definitely yes	22.8
Number of respondents	**327**

**Table C.29. Please tell us if each of these happened in the last 12 months:
Percent, except as noted**

Response	Rate
You or partner were turned down for credit	29.1
You or partner were not given as much credit as you applied for	14.9
You or partner put off applying because you thought you might be turned down	18.7
Number of respondents	**1,359**

**Table C.30. In the past 12 months, have you applied for a mortgage either to refinance an existing mortgage or to buy a home?
Percent, except as noted**

Response	Rate
Refused	1.7
No, have not applied for a mortgage to refinance or buy a home	86.0
Yes, to refinance	7.5
Yes, to buy a home	4.2
Yes to both refinance AND to buy a home	0.6
Number of respondents	**4,134**

Table C.31. If you were to apply for a mortgage today, how confident are you that your application would be approved? Percent, except as noted

Response	Rate
Refused	1.6
Very confident	33.9
Somewhat confident	18.6
Not confident	29.0
Don't know	16.9
Number of respondents	**4,134**

Table C.32. If it became easier to get approved for a mortgage than it is today, how likely is it that you would apply? Percent, except as noted

Response	Rate
Refused	0.6
Very unlikely	32.4
Somewhat unlikely	18.3
Somewhat likely	27.5
Very likely	21.2
Number of respondents	1,831

Table C.33. If you were to apply for credit or a loan today, how confident are you that your application would be approved? Percent, except as noted

Response	Rate
Refused	1.6
Very confident	41.2
Somewhat confident	21.3
Not confident	22.3
Don't know	13.5
Number of respondents	**4,134**

Table C.34. In the past 12 months have you had a lease application for an apartment or house denied because of your credit history? Percent, except as noted

Response	Rate
Refused	1.0
No	94.7
Yes	4.2
Number of respondents	**1,368**

Table C.35. If you had to guess, how would you rate your current credit score? Percent, except as noted

Response	Rate
Refused	1.4
Poor	11.6
Fair	11.7
Good	15.8
Very good	21.2
Excellent	25.0
Don't know my score or how to **rate** it	13.2
Number of respondents	**4,134**

Table C.36. In the past 12 months, have you:Percent, except as noted

Response	Rate
Obtained or received a copy of your credit report	31.5
Obtained or received your credit score	34.6
Number of respondents	**4,134**

Table C.37. In the past 12 months, have you always paid your credit card bills in full each month? Percent, except as noted

Response	Rate
Refused	0.4
No	43.0
Yes	56.6
Number of respondents	**3,263**

Table C.38. In the past 12 months, have you ever: Percent, except as noted

Response	Rate
Carried over a balance on your credit card and been charged interest	82.3
Paid only the minimum payment on one or more of your credit card bills	52.5
Carried a balance on your credit card at a low-interest rate from a special offer	41.9
Used a credit card for a cash advance	11.9
Number of respondents	**1,366**

Table C.39. If you've borrowed money for your own education, are you: Percent, except as noted

Response	Rate
Making payments on one of these loans now	50.8
One or more loans are in deferment/forbearance so do not	34.4
Behind on payments for one or more of these loans	16.3
One or more of these loans is in collections	8.6
Number of respondents	**568**

Table C.40. If you've borrowed money for your spouse's education, are you: Percent, except as noted

Response	Rate
Making payments on one of these loans now	67.3
One or more loans are in deferment/forbearance so do not	21.9
Behind on payments for one or more of these loans	11.0
One or more of these loans is in collections	6.1
Number of respondents	**278**

Table C.41. If you've borrowed money for your child's education, are you:Percent, except as noted

Response	Rate
Making payments on one of these loans now	50.9
One or more loans are in deferment/forbearance so do not	20.3
Behind on payments for one or more of these loans	8.6
One or more of these loans is in collections	3.9
Number of respondents	**290**

Table C.42. If you've borrowed money for your grandchild's education, are you: Percent, except as noted

Response	Rate
Making payments on one of these loans now	47.0
One or more loans are in deferment/forbearance so do not	13.6
Behind on payments for one or more of these loans	11.9
One or more of these loans is in collections	8.2
Number of respondents	**32**

Table C.43. Did you complete the most recent educational program for which you borrowed money? Percent, except as noted

Response	Rate
Refused	0.3
No	24.3
Yes	47.9
Still enrolled in the program	27.5
Number of respondents	**568**

Table C.44. Overall, how would you say the lifetime financial benefits of your most recent educational program compare to the lifetime financial costs to you of this education? Percent, except as noted

Response	Rate
Refused	0.3
Much larger financial benefits than costs	23.7
Somewhat larger financial benefits than costs	18.3
About same financial benefits and costs	21.0
Somewhat smaller financial benefits than costs	11.8
Much smaller financial benefits than costs	24.9
Number of respondents	**568**

Table C.45. Which one of the following broad categories best describes your major at the school you borrowed money to attend? Percent, except as noted

Response	Rate
Refused	1.2
Humanities	5.0
Social/behavioral sciences	6.4
Life sciences	4.0
Physical sciences/math	1.7
Computer/information sciences	6.6
Engineering	6.6
Education	10.1
Business/management	17.5
Health	15.6
Law	3.9
Vocational/technical training	4.3
Undeclared	3.0
Other (Please specify)	14.1
Number of respondents	**568**

Table C.46. Still thinking about your most recent educational program, what type of degree or credential did you borrow money for? Percent, except as noted

Response	Rate
Refused	0.4
Certificate or technical training	12.1
Associate's degree	15.5
Bachelor's degree	46.6
Master's degree	12.5
Professional degree (e.g., MBA, MD, JD)	5.2
Doctoral degree	4.7
Other (Please specify)	2.9
Number of respondents	**567**

Table C.47. Over the past 12 months, have you had to cut back on any spending so that you could make your monthly student loan payment? Percent, except as noted

Response	Rate
No	54.8
Yes, had to cut back a little	34.5
Yes, had to cut back a lot	10.7
Number of respondents	**586**

Table C.48. During the past 12 months, was there a time when you needed any of the following, but didn't get it because you couldn't afford it? Percent, except as noted

Response	Rate
Prescription medicine	14.9
To see a doctor	17.6
Mental health care or counseling	6.7
Dental care	25.7
To see a specialist	11.4
Follow-up care	10.3
Number of respondents	**4,134**

Table C.49. During the past 12 months, have you had any unexpected major medical expenses that you had to pay out of pocket? Percent, except as noted

Response	Rate
Refused	1.2
No	74.4
Yes	24.4
Number of respondents	**4,134**

Table C.50. If you were to have a major unexpected medical expense that you had to pay for out of pocket, how likely is it that you would be able to pay your medical bills? Percent, except as noted

Response	Rate
Refused	1.3
Not likely	42.8
Somewhat likely	34.5
Very likely	21.4
Number of respondents	**4,134**

Table C.51. Are you currently covered by any of the following types of health insurance or health coverage plans? Percent, except as noted

Response	Rate
Insurance through a current or former employer or union	52.5
Insurance purchased directly from an insurance company	13.2
Medicare, for people 65 or older, or people with certain disabilities	21.7
Medicaid	12.5
TRICARE or other military health care	3.5
VA	4.9
Indian Health Service	1.1
Other	4.9
Number of respondents	**4,134**

Table C.52. How much responsibility do you have for the following tasks? Paying monthly bills Percent, except as noted

Response	Rate
None or almost none	12.3
Some	10.0
Shared equally with other household members	21.7
Most	8.6
All or almost all	45.8
Number of respondents	**4,134**

Table C.53. Which one of the following best describes how well you are managing financially these days? Percent, except as noted

Response	Rate
Refused	1.1
Finding it very difficult to get by	13.3
Just getting by	25.3
Doing okay	37.3
Living comfortably	23.0
Number of respondents	**4,134**

Table C.54. Compared to five years ago (2008), would you say that you (and your family living with you) are better off, the same, or worse off financially? Percent, except as noted

Response	Rate
Refused	1.4
Much worse	12.4
Somewhat worse	22.0
About the same	34.2
Somewhat better off	20.0
Much better off	10.0
Number of respondents	**4,134**

Table C.55. How much thought have you given to the financial planning for your retirement? Percent, except as noted

Response	Rate
Refused	1.3
None at all	25.1
A little	23.8
Some	22.6
A fair amount	15.7
A lot	11.4
Number of respondents	**3,163**

Table C.56. Which one of the following best describes your plan for retirement? Percent, except as noted

Response	Rate
Refused	0.7
I do not plan to retire	6.2
Work fewer hours as I get close to retirement	9.6
Retire from my current career, but then find a different full-time job	3.8
Retire from my current career, but then find a different part-time job	15.8
Retire from my current career, but then work for myself	9.8
Work full time until I retire, then stop working altogether	25.4
Keep working as long as possible	21.3
Other (Please specify)	7.2
Number of respondents	**1,766**

Table C.57. Please tell us what types of retirement savings or pension you (or spouse) have: Percent, except as noted

Response	Rate
No retirement savings or pension	30.9
Social Security benefits	36.3
401(k), 403(b), Thrift or other defined contribution pension plan through an employer	43.7
Defined benefit pension through an employer	18.2
Individual Retirement Account (IRA)	23.0
Savings outside a retirement account	22.7
Real estate or land	11.3
Other	3.2
Refused	2.7
Number of respondents	**3,163**

Table C.58. How are you and your spouse planning to pay for expenses in retirement? Percent, except as noted

Response	Rate
Social Security Old-Age benefits	44.6
I will continue working	23.5
Spouse/partner will continue working	8.8
Defined benefit pension from work	18.5

Table C.58. (Continued)

Response	Rate
401(k), 403(b), thrift or other defined contribution pension plan from work	39.7
Individual Retirement Account (IRA)	22.1
Savings outside a retirement account	23.4
Income from real estate or the sale of real estate	8.3
Income from a business or the sale of a business	3.8
Rely on children, grandchildren, or other family	2.8
I don't know	24.6
Other	3.1
Refused	2.5
Number of respondents	**3,051**

Table C.59. Compared to your retirement plans before 2008, would you say that you now plan to retire: Percent, except as noted

Response	Rate
Refused	1.6
Plan to retire earlier	5.1
Plan to retire at the same age	33.1
Plan to retire later	35.7
Didn't think about retirement prior to 2008	24.4
Number of respondents	**1,766**

Table C.60. In the past 12 months, have you borrowed money from any of your retirement savings accounts? Percent, except as noted

Response	Rate
Refused	1.8
No	91.3
Yes	6.9
Number of respondents	**2,359**

Table C.61. In the past 12 months, have you cashed out any of your retirement savings? Percent, except as noted

Response	Rate
Refused	2.4
No	92.5
Yes	5.2
Number of respondents	**2,359**

Table C.62. Thinking about your retirement, tell us if any of the following happened to you: Percent, except as noted

Response	Rate
Worked fewer hours as I got close to retirement	15.4
Retired from my previous career, but then found a different full-time job	6.3
Retired from my previous career, but then found a different part-time job	13.8
Retired from my previous career, but then started working as self-employed	8.1
Worked full time until I retired, then stopped working altogether	57.6
Number of respondents	**971**

Table C.63. Are you (and your spouse) using any of these to pay for expenses in retirement? Percent, except as noted

Response	Rate
Social Security Old-Age benefits	74.5
I have a job	5.8
My spouse/partner has a job	11.9
Defined benefit pension from work	44.3
401(k), 403(b), thrift or other defined contribution pension plan from work	18.5
Individual Retirement Account (IRA)	28.8
Savings outside a retirement account	31.6
Income from real estate or the sale of real estate	8.8
Income from a business or the sale of a business	2.6
Relying on children, grandchildren, or other family	1.9
Other	5.9
Refused	5.8
Number of respondents	**971**

Table C.64. Did the recent recession affect your decision to retire? Percent, except as noted

Response	Rate
Refused	0.8
No	79.6
Yes, retired earlier than planned	15.1
Yes, retired later than planned	4.5
Number of respondents	**314**

Table C.65. Since 2008, have you or your family living with you experienced any significant major life change or financial hardship? Percent, except as noted

Response	Rate
Refused	1.8
No	56.6
Yes	41.6
Number of respondents	**4,134**

Table C.66. Which of the following did your family experience since 2008? Percent, except as noted

Response	Rate
I lost a job	33.9
I had my work hours and/or pay reduced	23.5
My spouse/partner lost a job	20.2
My spouse/partner had their work hours and/or pay reduced	13.4
Received a foreclosure notice	7.1
A business I owned had financial difficulty	5.9
Had a health emergency	30.5
Divorce	8.5
Had a baby	9.9
Death of primary breadwinner	3.5
Other	16.8
Refused	2.2
Number of respondents	**1,680**

Table C.67. Did you delay any major expenses or purchases because of the recession that began in 2008?
Percent, except as noted

Response	Rate
Refused	1.9
No	56.6
Yes	41.5
Number of respondents	**4,134**

Table C.68. What major purchase did you delay?
Percent, except as noted

Response	Rate
Buying a home	20.5
Buying a car	56.6
Buying a major appliance	30.7
Going on vacation	66.9
Home improvements	44.4
Other	4.9
Refused	0.2
Number of respondents	**1,694**

Table C.69. Did you delay any major life decisions because of the recession that began in 2008?
Percent, except as noted

Response	Rate
Refused	2.1
No	79.6
Yes	18.4
Number of respondents	**4,134**

Table C.70. What major life decisions did you delay?
Percent, except as noted

Response	Rate
Marriage	15.3
Retirement	16.4
Having a child	17.7
Buying a home	45.0
Moving to new city or state	34.1
Changing jobs	21.1
Other	9.3
Refused	1.5
Number of respondents	**709**

Table C.71. Before 2008, did you or your household have any savings?
Percent, except as noted

Response	Rate
Refused	1.9
No	27.1
Yes	61.1
Don't know	10.0
Number of respondents	**4,134**

Table C.72. Since 2008, have you or your household had to use up some, nearly all, or all of your savings to pay for bills and expenses?
Percent, except as noted

Response	Rate
Refused	0.7
No	42.0
Yes, some	31.9
Yes, nearly all	12.3
Yes, all	13.1
Number of respondents	**2,845**

Table C.73. Since 2008, have you or your household received any financial assistance from your family or a friend?
Percent, except as noted

Response	Rate
Refused	2.2
No	76.1
Yes	21.7
Number of respondents	**4,134**

Table C.74. Since 2008, have you or your household provided any financial assistance to a friend or a family member?
Percent, except as noted

Response	Rate
Refused	2.1
No	63.5
Yes	34.4
Number of respondents	**4,134**

Table C.75. Thinking about your current education and work experience, how confident are you that you have the skills necessary to get the kinds of jobs you want now?
Percent, except as noted

Response	Rate
Refused	1.8
Very confident	27.3
Somewhat confident	39.2
Not confident	18.3
I am not currently in the workforce and I am not looking for a job	6.9
Don't know	6.5
Number of respondents	**2,864**

Table C.76. Thinking about the types of jobs you believe will be available in ten years, how confident are you that you have the skills necessary to get the kinds of jobs you want?
Percent, except as noted

Response	Rate
Refused	2.1
Very confident	23.2
Somewhat confident	38.8
Not confident	19.2
I do not expect to be working 10 years from now	8.0
Don't know	8.7
Number of respondents	**2,864**

Table C.77. Why a lack of confidence for jobs today?
Percent, except as noted

Response	Rate
I need more education or another degree	49.4
I need more job training	39.8
My skills are out of date because I haven't been using them	20.4
The job market is changing faster than I can keep up with	25.4
The kind of job I'm qualified for is not available	21.3
Refused	1.0
Number of respondents	**295**

Table C.78. Why a lack of confidence for jobs in 10 years?
Percent, except as noted

Response	Rate
I will need more education or another degree to be competitive	41.1
I will need more job training to be competitive	47.7
My skills will be out of date in ten years	36.8
The job market will change faster than I can keep up with	35.9
The kind of job I'm qualified for may not be available in 10 years	22.7
Refused	0.8
Number of respondents	**368**

Table C.79. In 2012, would you say that your household's total spending was more, the same, or less than your income? Percent, except as noted

Response	Rate
Refused	2.2
Spending was less than income	37.7
Spending was same as income	38.4
Spending was more than income	21.7
Number of respondents	**4,134**

Table C.80. Which of the following categories are you saving money for? Percent, except as noted

Response	Rate
Education (yours or someone else's)	17.9
Retirement	58.0
Your children	20.5
Major appliance, car, or other big purchase (excluding a home)	20.4
Home purchase	13.0
Pay off debts	26.5
Unexpected expenses	52.6
Just to save	49.1
Taxes	15.0
To leave behind some inheritance or charitable donation	10.6
Other	4.9
Refused	0.7
Number of respondents	**2,270**

Table C.81. Which of the following categories best describes your total household income from all sources, before taxes and deductions in 2012? Percent, except as noted

Response	Rate
Refused	35.4
$0 to $4,999	4.7
$5,000 to $14,999	8.4
$15,000 to $24,999	5.3
$25,000 to $49,999	18.0
$50,000 to $74,999	9.5

Table C.81. (Continued)

Response	Rate
$75,000 to $99,999	7.8
$100,000 to $149,999	6.6
$150,000 to $199,999	2.1
$200,000 to $249,000	0.5
$250,000 or higher	1.6
Number of respondents	**493**

Table C.82. Was your total household income in 2012 higher or lower compared to what you would expect in a normal year?
Percent, except as noted

Response	Rate
Refused	3.1
Low	29.9
Normal	59.7
High	7.3
Number of respondents	**4,134**

Table C.83. Which of the following categories best describes your total household income in a normal year?
Percent, except as noted

Response	Rate
Refused	32.2
$0 to $4,999	12.4
$5,000 to $14,999	12.2
$15,000 to $24,999	8.7
$25,000 to $49,999	15.4
$50,000 to $74,999	7.3
$75,000 to $99,999	2.5
$100,000 to $149,999	3.9
$150,000 to $199,999	1.7
$200,000 to $249,000	1.4
$250,000 or higher	2.4
Number of respondents	**154**

Table C.84. During the next 12 months, do you expect your total income to be higher, about the same or lower than during the past 12 months? Percent, except as noted

Response	Rate
Refused	2.7
Lower	16.1
About the same	60.5
Higher	20.7
Number of respondents	**4,134**

Table C.85. Which one of the following best describes how your household's income changes from month to month, if at all? Percent, except as noted

Response	Rate
Refused	3.1
Roughly the same amount each month	66.1
Roughly the same most months, but some unusually high or low months during the year	20.6
Often varies quite a bit from one month to the next	10.1
Number of respondents	**4,134**

Table C.86. Why does your income change from month to month? Percent, except as noted

Response	Rate
Bonuses	12.4
Commissions	6.9
Seasonal employment	12.0
Irregular work schedule	41.6
Periods of unemployment	14.7
Investment Income	9.2
Other	23.3
Refused	4.3
Number of respondents	**1,225**

Table C.87. If you were to lose your main source of income (e.g., job, government benefits), could you cover your expenses for 3 months by borrowing money, using savings, selling assets, or borrowing from friends/family? Percent, except as noted

Response	Rate
Refused	2.2
No	42.2
Yes	55.6
Number of respondents	**2,136**

Table C.88. Have you set aside emergency or rainy day funds that would cover your expenses for 3 months in case of sickness, job loss, economic downturn, or other emergencies? Percent, except as noted

Response	Rate
Refused	2.7
No	57.9
Yes	39.4
Number of respondents	**1,998**

Table C.89. Suppose that you have an emergency expense that costs $400. Based on your current financial situation how would you pay for this expense? If you would use more than one method to cover this expense please select all that apply Percent, except as noted

Response	Rate
Put it on my credit card and pay it off in full	
at the next statement	27.7
Put it on my credit card and pay it off over time	16.9
With the money currently in my checking/savings account or with cash	38.6
Using money from a bank loan or line of credit	3.2
By borrowing from a friend or family member	11.8
Using a payday loan, deposit advance, or overdraft	3.6
By selling something	9.5
I wouldn't be able to pay for the expense right now	18.9
Other	2.1
Refused	2.9
Number of respondents	**4,134**

Table C.90. Do you regularly set aside part of any income you receive in some type of savings account? Percent, except as noted

Response	Rate
Refused	1.3
No	47.1
Yes	51.6
Number of respondents	**3,816**

Table C.91. Which one of these is the main reason that you play lotteries or other types of gambling? Percent, except as noted

Response	Rate
Refused	1.5
For the money or prizes	55.0
As a pastime or for entertainment	33.9
As a form of charitable donation	3.6
Other (Please specify)	5.9
Number of respondents	**2,063**

Table C.92. During the past 12 months, about how much money would you say that you spent on state lotteries or other types of gambling? Percent, except as noted

Response	Rate
Refused	1.4
Less than $100	66.0
$100 to $249	16.2
$250 to $499	7.2
More than $500	6.4
Don't know	2.7
Number of respondents	**2,063**

Table C.93. In a typical year, about how often do you buy or sell stocks in individual companies, including trades in a retirement account like a 401(k)? Percent, except as noted

Response	Rate
Refused	6.5
Buy or sell at least once a week	3.2
Buy or sell at least once a month	8.7
Buy or sell at least once a quarter	12.9
Buy or sell at least once a year	14.6
Buy or sell less than once a year	54.1
Number of respondents	**1,559**

Table C.94. Which one of the following statements comes closest to describing the amount of financial risk that you are willing to take when you save or make investments? Percent, except as noted

Response	Rate
Refused	3.1
Take substantial financial risks expecting to earn substantial returns	4.4
Take above average financial risks expecting to earn above average returns	13.0
Take average financial risks expecting to earn average returns	31.4
Not willing to take any financial risks	48.2
Number of respondents	**4,134**

Table C.95. Suppose that you are the only income earner in the family. You have to choose between the following two jobs. Which job would you take? Percent, except as noted

Response	Rate
Refused	2.8
This job would guarantee your current total family income for life.	82.1
This job is better paying, but the income is also less certain. There is a 50-50 chance this job would double your total lifetime income and a 50-50 chance that it would cut it by a third.	15.1
Number of respondents	**4,134**

Table C.96. Now which job would you take? Percent, except as noted

Response	Rate
Refused	1.0
This job would guarantee your current total family income for life.	80.6
This job is better paying, but the income is also less certain. Suppose the chances were 50-50 that this job would double your lifetime income and 50-50 that it would cut it by 20 percent.	18.5
Number of respondents	**3,411**

Table C.97. Now which job would you take? Percent, except as noted

Response	Rate
Refused	2.3
This job would guarantee your current total family income for life.	38.2
Suppose the chances were 50-50 that this job would double your lifetime income and 50-50 that it would cut it by half.	59.5
Number of respondents	**621**

Table C.98. Now which job would you take? Percent, except as noted

Response	Rate
Refused	0.8
This job would guarantee your current total family income for life.	52.2
Suppose the chances were 50-50 that this job would double your lifetime income and 50-50 that it would cut it by 75 percent.	47.0
Number of respondents	**356**

Table C.99. Now which job would you take? Percent, except as noted

Response	Rate
Refused	2.0
This job would guarantee your current total family income for life.	66.5
Suppose the chances were 50-50 that this job would double your lifetime income and 50-50 that it would cut it by 10 percent.	31.5
Number of respondents	2,772

Summary Statistics

Table C.100. Summary statistics for numeric questions

	Mean	Median	Observations
How many credit cards do you have?	2.5	2	4,080
At what age did you retire fully, meaning completely stop working?	61.3	62	759
About how much do you pay for rent each month?	829.8	700	959
In what year did you buy your current home?	1,998.3	2,002	2,692
For your education: number of loans	2.7	2	540
For your spouse's/partner's education: number of loans	1.9	1	260
For your child's education: number of loans	1.6	1	264
For your grandchild's education: number of loans	1.3	1	29
For your education: total $ amount owed	25,749.9	13,000	514
For your spouse's/partner's education: total $ amount owed	24,592.9	12,000	237
For your child's education: total $ amount owed	14,923.3	8,000	233
For your grandchild's education: total $ amount owed	16,090.1	6,000	20
For your education: total $ amount of monthly payment on these loans	245.2	160	352
For your spouse's/partner's education: total $ amount of monthly payment on these loans	241.8	200	198
For your grandchild's education: total $ amount of monthly payment on these loans	208.7	138	19
In what year did you complete the program that you borrowed the money for?	2,006.8	2,009	276
Among non-retirees: on a scale of 1–10, what are the chances that you will live to age 75?	7.0	8	3,073

	Mean	Median	Observations
Among non-retirees: on a scale of 1 10, what are the chances that you will live to age 85?	5.4	5	3,063
Among retirees under 75: On a scale of 1–10, what are the chances that you will live to age 75?	8.1	9	696
Among retirees under 85: On a scale of 1–10, what are the chances that you will live to age 85?	6.4	7	913
In 2012, about what percentage of your income did your household set aside as savings?	8.5	2	3,920
How much was the total income your household received in 2012 from all sources, before taxes and deductions?	62,645.8	42,000	3,641
What would you say your total household income is in a normal year?	58,145.7	40,000	1,289
If you received $1,000 in unexpected income today, how much of it would you spend?	227.4	100	3,909
If you received $1,000 in unexpected income today, how much of it would you save?	395.3	300	3,909
If you received $1,000 in unexpected income today, how much of it would you use to pay down existing debt?	377.3	250	3,909
Age	46.8	47	4,134

Table C.101. Summary statistics for demographics (unweighted)

	Mean	Standard deviation	Observations
Age	49.9927	16.7869	4,134
Male	0.5077	0.5000	4,134
Female	0.4923	0.5000	4,134
18–29	0.1555	0.3625	4,134
30–44	0.2184	0.4132	4,134
45–60	0.3246	0.4683	4,134
Ages over 60	0.3014	0.4589	4,134
Less than high school	0.0796	0.2707	4,134

Table C.101. (Continued)

	Mean	Standard deviation	Observations
High school degree	0.2910	0.4543	4,134
Some college	0.2929	0.4552	4,134
Bachelor's degree or higher	0.3365	0.4726	4,134
White, non-Hispanic	0.7361	0.4408	4,134
Black, non-Hispanic	0.0902	0.2865	4,134
Other, non-Hispanic	0.0336	0.1803	4,134
Hispanic	0.1035	0.3047	4,134
2 or more races, non-Hispanic	0.0365	0.1876	4,134
Less than $25,000	0.2453	0.4303	3,921
$25,000–$39,999	0.2193	0.4138	3,921
$40,000–$74,999	0.1895	0.3919	3,921
$75,000–$99,999	0.1316	0.3381	3,921
Greater than $100,000	0.2142	0.4103	3,921
Married	0.5578	0.4967	4,134
Not married	0.4422	0.4967	4,134
Northeast	0.1904	0.3926	4,134
Midwest	0.2300	0.4209	4,134
South	0.3551	0.4786	4,134
West	0.2245	0.4173	4,134
Employed	0.5554	0.4970	4,134
Unemployed, in labor force	0.0789	0.2696	4,134
Not in labor force	0.3657	0.4817	4,134

End Notes

[1] For more information on the SCF or to access SCF data, see www.federalreserve.gov/econresdata/scf/scfindex.htm.

[2] Sentences in which the respondent mention any of the terms retire, pensions, old age, Medicare, Supplemental Security Income, IRAs, 401(k), or Social Security were grouped into the "retirement" theme. Those that mentioned any of the terms college, school, education, tuition, degree, or university were grouped into the "education" theme. The "employment" theme included any mention of the terms jobs, employment, employed, laid off, part time, hours, full time, cutback, and skills.

[3] U.S. Census Bureau (2013), "Residential Vacancies and Homeownership in the Third Quarter 2013," news release, November 5, www.census.gov/housing/hvs/files/qtr313/q313press.pdf.

[4] Respondents were not able to report negative levels of savings if they are borrowing to spend more than their income or spending out of their savings. As a result, the average level of

savings for the population may be less than the 8 percent reported once these dissavers are included.

[5] The 90 percent of respondents with a checking, savings, or money market account is consistent with the Federal Deposit Insurance Corporation's estimate that 92 percent of individuals have a bank account of some kind. See www.fdic.gov/householdsurvey/ 2012_ unbankedreport.pdf.

[6] Among married couples, the fraction reporting a student loan for themselves (12 percent) is almost identical to the fraction reporting a student loan for their spouse (11 percent).

[7] Respondents were asked about debt used to pay for education, which includes traditional student loans (e.g., Stafford loans), but for some respondents this debt could also include sources such as credit cards or home equity lines of credit if used to pay education bills. For the purposes of discussion in this section, this debt, regardless of specific source, is also referred to as student loan debt.

[8] These figures also do not represent the total debt incurred for the education, since respondents may have paid off a portion of the loan since completing the degree, reducing the balance, or may have had interest accrue on the loan, increasing the balance. Furthermore, while respondents were asked about all student loan debt, they were only asked to provide information about the most recent school that they borrowed money to attend. Therefore, if a respondent borrowed money to attend multiple schools, it is not possible to determine what portion of the total debt was acquired for a particular school.

[9] For a summary of how the distribution of such plans has changed over time, see www.dol.gov/ebsa/pdf/historicaltables.pdf.

[10] The regression results also indicate that greater age, higher education levels, and being married are significant predictors of planning for retirement.

[11] It is possible that the percent reporting Social Security utilization may be undercounted due to the way the question was specified. The question asks, in the present tense, "...what types of retirement savings or pension [do] you (or your spouse) have?" One of the options is "Social Security benefits." While the question and option were meant to understand the percentage of respondents who anticipated relying on Social Security in retirement, the construction may have led some respondents to answer in the negative because they were not currently receiving benefits. Forty-five percent of respondents said that they were "planning to" use Social Security benefits to pay for retirement, but only 36 percent reported that they "have" Social Security benefits. According to the Social Security Administration, nine out of ten individuals age 65 or older currently receive Social Security benefits. See www.ssa.gov/pressoffice/basicfact.htm.

[12] U.S. Census Bureau (2013), "Health Insurance Coverage Status," factfinder2.census.gov/faces/ tableservices/jsf/pages/table.

[13] These factors are statistically significant predictors of the respondent reporting that he or she had avoided some form of medical treatment due to cost, even after accounting for income and age in a probit regression.

[14] For further details on the KnowledgePanel sampling methodology and comparisons between KnowledgePanel and telephone surveys, see www.knowledgenetworks.com/accuracy/ spring2010/disogra-spring10.html.

[15] David S. Yeager, Jon A. Krosnick, LinChiat Chang, Harold S. Javitz, Matthew S. Levendusky, Alberto Simpser, and Rui Wang (2011) "Comparing the Accuracy of RDD Telephone Surveys and Internet Surveys Conducted with Probability and NonProbability Samples," Public Opinion Quarterly, vol. 75(4), pp. 709–47.

In: 2013 Economic Well-Being
Editor: Barry Sutton

ISBN: 978-1-63463-118-1

Chapter 2

SUPPLEMENTAL APPENDIX TO THE REPORT ON THE ECONOMIC WELL-BEING OF U.S. HOUSEHOLDS IN 2013*

Maximilian D. Schmeiser, David E. Buchholz, Alexandra M. Brown, Matthew B. Gross, Jeff H. Larrimore, Ellen A. Merry, Barbara J. Robles and Logan M. Thomas

SUPPLEMENTAL TABLES BY DEMOGRAPHIC AND SOCIOECONOMIC CHARACTERISTICS

The tables in this appendix contain supplemental information from the Survey of Household Economics and Decisionmaking (SHED). The appendix provides additional information about select questions from each main section of the *Report on the EconomicWell-Being of U.S. Households in 2013*, which summarizes the SHED results. For each question included in this appendix, information is reported about the distribution of certain demographic and socioeconomic factors, namely the respondents' race/ethnicity, age, gender, income, and education.

---

* This appendix (issued July 2014) was prepared by the Consumer and Community Development Research Section of the Federal Reserve Board's Division of Consumer and Community Affairs (DCCA).

Web Table 1. Responses to overall financial well-being questions (by race/ethnicity)
Percent, except as noted

	Race/ethnicity				
	Non-Hispanic white	Non-Hispanic black	Hispanic	Overall	N
Which one of the following best describes how well you are managing financially these days?					
Finding it difficult to get by	12.2	17.3	15.7	13.3	462
Just getting by	23.5	30.7	30.0	25.3	970
Doing okay	37.7	37.2	35.2	37.3	1,578
Living comfortably	25.5	13.7	18.0	23.0	1,088
Compared to five years ago (2008), would you say that you are better off, the same, or worse off financially?					
Much worse	12.4	12.3	11.9	12.4	469
Somewhat worse	24.1	16.4	18.7	22.0	945
About the same	33.2	36.4	34.7	34.2	1,462
Somewhat better off	20.0	20.2	20.2	20.0	849
Much better off	9.0	12.9	12.8	10.0	368
During the next 12 months, do you expect your total income to be higher, about the same, or lower than during the past 12 months?					
Lower	15.4	19.4	13.8	16.1	689
About the same	62.3	53.9	61.5	60.5	2,559
Higher	19.8	21.9	22.4	20.7	802

Note: Questions were asked of all respondents, except as noted.

Web Table 2. Responses to housing questions (by race/ethnicity)
Percent, except as noted

	Race/ethnicity				
	Non-Hispanic white	Non-Hispanic black	Hispanic	Overall	N
Please select all the reason below for why you rent your home rather than own your home? (asked of renters)					
It's cheaper to rent than own a home	21.7	23.0	27.5	22.8	232

	Race/ethnicity				
	Non-Hispanic white	Non-Hispanic black	Hispanic	Overall	N
It's more convenient to rent (for example, you can move easily)	26.0	21.1	24.9	24.4	259
I plan on moving in the near future	19.8	17.5	24.4	20.1	212
I can't qualify for a mortgage to buy a home	29.6	29.5	29.7	29.1	291
I can't afford the down payment to buy a home	42.1	46.8	51.5	45.3	444
I simply prefer to rent	19.3	22.8	18.6	19.6	207
I'm currently looking to buy a home	11.9	10.5	5.2	9.7	104
Other	10.5	6.9	6.2	8.9	112
Compared to five years ago (since 2008), do you think the value of your home today is higher, lower, or stayed the same? (asked of homeowners)					
Lower value	46.8	37.4	46.3	45.2	981
Value has stayed the same	21.1	12.5	15.0	19.5	479
Higher value	24.6	31.2	33.5	26.9	599
Don't Know	6.9	15.0	4.8	7.5	148
In the next 12 months, how much, if at all, do you think that home prices in your neighborhood will change? (asked of homeowners)					
Go down by more than 5 percent	3.1	5.9	2.8	3.4	92
Go down by 5 percent or less	4.6	4.7	6.4	4.9	122
Stay about the same	40.3	23.4	33.0	36.8	1,046
Go up by 5 percent or less	24.9	22.3	31.4	25.8	734
Go up by more than 5 percent	12.1	15.9	16.4	13.5	351
Don't know	14.7	26.3	9.6	15.1	377
Thinking about the past 12 months, did you want to sell your home, but did not or could not? (asked of homeowners)					
Yes, I put it on the market, but could not sell it	1.9	1.3	2.3	1.9	45
Yes, I wanted to sell, but did not put it on the market	8.4	12.2	10.8	9.1	232
No, I did not want to sell	86.4	82.1	82.4	85.6	2,378
No, I was able to sell my home, or it's currently on the market	2.7	0.0	2.9	2.5	61

Note: Questions were asked of all respondents, except as noted.

Web Table 3. Responses to credit behavior and availability questions (by race/ethnicity)
Percent, except as noted

	Race/ethnicity				
	Non-Hispanic white	Non-Hispanic black	Hispanic	Overall	N
In the past 12 months, have you put off applying for credit because you thought you might be turned down?					
No	83.3	69.0	70.3	79.5	3,394
Yes	15.2	28.7	26.8	18.7	676
If you were to apply for a mortgage today, how confident are you that your application would be approved?					
Confident	57.3	37.7	42.2	52.5	2,427
Not confident	27.0	32.6	37.2	29.0	1,056
Don't know	14.2	28.0	18.3	16.9	601
If you were to apply for credit or a loan today (other than a mortgage), how confident are you that your application would be approved?					
Very confident	48.2	20.8	26.5	41.2	1,973
Somewhat confident	19.5	24.5	27.2	21.3	835
Not confident	19.5	28.0	30.7	22.3	787
Don't know	11.2	24.5	13.9	13.5	486
If you had to guess, how would you rate your current credit score (such as a FICO score)?					
Poor	9.8	18.6	15.8	11.6	397
Fair	10.1	16.9	16.4	11.7	419
Good	14.1	16.3	25.1	15.8	607
Very good	24.0	9.4	14.9	21.2	950
Excellent	30.6	10.9	12.3	25.0	1,271
Don't know my score or how to rate it	10.3	24.8	13.9	13.2	446
In the past 12 months, have you always paid your credit card bills in full each month? (asked of respondents with at least one credit card)					
No	41.7	52.0	51.3	43.0	1,366
Yes	57.8	47.4	48.7	56.6	1,886

Note: Questions were asked of all respondents, except as noted.

Web Table 4. Responses to savings behavior questions (by race/ethnicity) Percent, except as noted

	Race/ethnicity				
	Non-Hispanic white	Non-Hispanic black	Hispanic	Overall	N
In 2012, would you say that your household's total spending was more than your income, that it or that you spent less than your income?					
Spending was less than income	39.8	36.8	27.8	37.7	1,622
Spending was same as income	37.7	36.3	41.6	38.4	1,589
Spending was more than income	20.2	24.6	28.7	21.7	850
If you were to lose your main source of income (e.g., job, government benefits), could you cover your expenses for 3 months by borrowing money, using savings, selling assets, or borrowing from friends/family? (asked of approximately one-half of respondents)					
No	38.0	59.0	54.0	42.2	805
Yes	59.7	38.5	44.3	55.6	1,291
Have you set aside emergency or rainy day funds that would cover your expenses for 3 months in case of sickness, job loss, economic downturn, or other emergencies? (asked of approximately one-half of respondents)					
No	53.8	72.1	63.3	57.9	1,055
Yes	43.4	26.6	32.9	39.4	899
Suppose that you have an emergency expense that costs $400. *Based on your current financial situation*, how would you pay for this expense? If you would use more than one method to cover this expense please select all that apply.					
Put it on my credit card and pay it off in full at the next statement	30.8	12.4	19.6	27.7	1,288
Put it on my credit card and pay it off over time	17.5	9.2	21.1	16.9	704
With the money currently in my checking/savings account or with cash	42.6	30.5	30.3	38.6	1,740
Using money from a bank loan or line of credit	3.0	2.5	3.9	3.2	138

Web Table 4. (Continued)

	Race/ethnicity				
	Non-Hispanic white	Non-Hispanic black	Hispanic	Overall	N
By borrowing from a friend or family member	9.9	17.4	15.3	11.8	411
Using a payday loan, deposit advance, or overdraft	2.0	7.6	7.4	3.6	117
By selling something	8.6	12.9	10.6	9.5	351
I wouldn't be able to pay for the expense right now	15.4	37.4	22.8	18.9	628
Other	2.3	2.1	1.9	2.1	86

Note: Questions were asked of all respondents, except as noted.

Web Table 5. Responses to education and student loan questions (by race/ethnicity)
Percent, except as noted

	Race/ethnicity				
	Non-Hispanic white	Non-Hispanic black	Hispanic	Overall	N
Do you currently owe any money or have any loans that you used to pay for your own education?					
No	72.5	56.3	61.7	68.6	2,977
Yes	13.4	21.8	21.5	15.8	568
Does not apply	12.9	20.2	14.8	14.2	537
Do you currently owe any money or have any loans that you used to pay for your own education, your spouse's education, your child's education, or your grandchild's education? [constructed]					
No	77.6	73.7	70.3	75.8	3,177
Yes	22.4	26.3	29.7	24.2	957

	Race/ethnicity				
	Non-Hispanic white	**Non-Hispanic black**	**Hispanic**	**Overall**	**N**
Did you complete the most recent educational program for which you borrowed money? (asked of respondents with debt for their own education)					
No	20.9	30.4	29.3	24.3	139
Yes	52.6	37.9	44.3	47.9	281
Still enrolled in the program	26.5	31.8	24.9	27.5	146
Overall, how would you say the lifetime *financial benefits* of your most recent educational program compare to the lifetime *financial costs* to you of this education? (asked of respondents with debt for their own education)					
Much larger financial benefits than costs	24.3	26.0	22.7	23.7	128
Somewhat larger financial benefits than costs	15.7	22.0	22.6	18.3	106
About same financial benefits and costs	21.0	28.8	12.7	21.0	118
Somewhat smaller financial benefits than costs	11.1	5.7	18.6	11.8	69
Much smaller financial benefits than costs	27.5	17.1	23.5	24.9	143
Thinking about your current education and work experience, how confident are you that you have the skills necessary to get the kinds of jobs you want *now*? (asked of respondents who are not retired or disabled)					
Very confident	27.4	32.4	28.3	27.3	829
Somewhat confident	39.5	29.6	41.2	39.2	1,126
Not confident	19.5	12.7	17.1	18.3	517
I am not currently in the workforce and I am not looking for a job	6.2	7.5	7.2	6.9	187
Don't know	5.6	17.0	3.6	6.5	162

Note: Questions were asked of all respondents, except as noted.

Web Table 6. Responses to retirement questions (by race/ethnicity) Percent, except as noted

	Race/ethnicity				
	Non-Hispanic white	Non-Hispanic black	Hispanic	Overall	N
How much thought have you given to the financial planning for your retirement? (asked of all respondents net yet retired)					
None at all	20.5	37.4	31.9	25.1	656
A little	23.5	18.9	27.1	23.8	705
Some	24.2	20.3	20.8	22.6	752
A fair amount	18.0	12.5	11.2	15.7	591
A lot	12.5	9.8	7.2	11.4	423
Which one of the following best describes your plan for retirement? (asked of all respondents net yet retired who have done some planning for retirement)					
I do not plan to retire	6.6	8.3	2.7	6.2	112
Work fewer hours as I get close to retirement	9.7	6.0	11.4	9.6	159
Retire from my current career, but then find a different full-time job	3.5	9.1	2.8	3.8	63
Retire from my current career, but then find a different part-time job	16.6	10.0	15.1	15.8	304
Retire from my current career, but then work for myself	7.8	14.5	15.0	9.8	171
Work full time until I retire, then stop working altogether	27.2	21.6	23.1	25.4	434
Keep working as long as possible	21.3	23.8	17.7	21.3	373
Other	6.8	6.6	9.4	7.2	140
What type of retirement savings do you have? (asked of all respondents net yet retired)					
No retirement savings or pension	25.4	42.5	40.0	30.9	804
Social Security Old-Age benefits	39.5	32.3	29.6	36.3	1,318
401(k), 403(b), thrift or other defined contribution pension plan	48.1	29.9	36.1	43.7	1,508
Defined benefit pension through an employer	20.7	13.8	12.1	18.2	725

	Race/ethnicity				
	Non-Hispanic white	Non-Hispanic black	Hispanic	Overall	N
Individual Retirement Account (IRA)	28.0	12.0	12.2	23.0	874
Savings outside a retirement account (e.g., a brokerage account, savings account)	27.0	11.6	13.4	22.7	862
Real estate or land	13.6	4.5	5.8	11.3	463
Other	3.3	3.8	2.6	3.2	87
How are you planning to pay for your expenses in retirement? (asked of non-retired respondents who plan to retire and who have done some planning for retirement)					
Social Security Old-Age benefits	49.9	34.6	35.6	44.6	1,553
I will continue working	25.2	19.2	21.9	23.5	758
Spouse/partner will continue working	9.6	6.2	7.6	8.8	296
Defined benefit pension from work	20.7	16.4	11.8	18.5	708
401(k), 403(b), thrift or other defined contribution pension plan from work	44.3	30.1	29.9	39.7	1,321
Individual Retirement Account (IRA)	27.1	11.7	12.4	22.1	809
Savings outside a retirement account (e.g., a brokerage account, savings account)	27.7	14.5	11.5	23.4	832
Income from real estate or the sale of real estate	8.8	4.9	7.7	8.3	296
Income from a business or the sale of a business	3.7	3.3	4.9	3.8	137
Rely on children, grandchildren, or other family	2.4	3.9	3.8	2.8	79
I don't know	20.8	33.0	29.9	24.6	631
Other	3.7	0.6	2.8	3.1	94
What sources are you (and your spouse/partner) using to pay for your expenses in retirement? (asked of all respondents who are currently retired)					
Social Security Old-Age benefits	75.8	69.3	61.0	74.5	730
I have a job	6.1	4.6	5.9	5.8	64
My spouse/partner has a job	12.2	11.9	9.4	11.9	120
Defined benefit pension from work	45.2	38.9	41.8	44.3	470

Web Table 6. (Continued)

	Race/ethnicity				
	Non-Hispanic white	Non-Hispanic black	Hispanic	Overall	N
401(k), 403(b), thrift or other defined contribution pension plan from work	19.0	10.0	18.0	18.5	210
Individual Retirement Account (IRA)	31.1	12.6	21.0	28.8	319
Savings outside a retirement account (e.g., a brokerage account, savings account)	35.0	6.4	21.0	31.6	335
Income from real estate or the sale of real estate	10.0	0.8	8.4	8.8	90
Income from a business or the sale of a business	3.1	0.0	0.0	2.6	28
Relying on children, grandchildren, or other family	2.2	0.0	1.0	1.9	16
Other	5.5	2.7	8.0	5.9	48

Note: Questions were asked of all respondents, except as noted.

Web Table 7. Responses to health insurance and health-care expenses questions (by race/ethnicity)
Percent, except as noted

	Race/ethnicity				
	Non-Hispanic white	Non-Hispanic black	Hispanic	Overall	N
During the past 12 months, was there a time when you needed any of the following, but didn't					
Prescription medicine (including taking less medication than prescribed)	14.2	18.5	17.1	14.9	532
To see a doctor	16.7	18.8	22.4	17.6	634
Mental health care or counseling	5.6	7.5	11.8	6.7	232

	Race/ethnicity				
	Non-Hispanic white	Non-Hispanic black	Hispanic	Overall	N
Dental care (including check-ups or routine cleaning)	24.9	32.2	28.7	25.7	972
To see a specialist (such as an OB/GYN, dermatologist, orthopedic surgeon, etc.)	11.5	10.4	14.1	11.4	427
Follow-up care (e.g., going to physical therapy sessions recommended by a doctor)	9.9	12.2	11.8	10.3	367
Any medical treatment listed above [constructed]	33.1	39.4	37.0	33.8	1,272
During the past 12 months, have you had any unexpected major medical expenses that you had to pay out of pocket (that were not completely paid for by insurance)?					
No	74.3	70.5	74.3	74.4	3,060
Yes	24.6	28.2	23.9	24.4	1,035
If you were to have a major unexpected medical expense that you had to pay for out of pocket, how likely is it that you that you would be able to pay your medical bills?					
Not likely	39.1	53.7	52.4	42.8	1,596
Somewhat likely	35.6	31.4	30.9	34.5	1,455
Very likely	24.0	13.1	15.1	21.4	1,041
Are you currently covered by any of the following types of health insurance or health coverage plans?					
Insurance through a current or former employer or union (of yourself or a family member)	56.7	39.0	41.8	52.5	2,336
Insurance purchased directly from an insurance company (by yourself or a family member)	14.5	10.1	11.0	13.2	580
Medicare, for people 65 or older, or people with certain disabilities	24.2	19.1	15.2	21.7	1,041
Medicaid, Medical Assistance, or any kind of government-assistance plan for those with low incomes or disability	9.0	23.9	19.3	12.5	406

Web Table 7. (Continued)

	Race/ethnicity				
	Non-Hispanic white	Non-Hispanic black	Hispanic	Overall	N
TRICARE or other military health care	3.1	3.9	5.4	3.5	161
VA (including those who have ever used or enrolled for VA health care)	4.6	7.0	4.9	4.9	223
Indian Health Service	0.3	0.6	1.7	1.1	31
Any other type of health insurance or health coverage plan	4.3	4.7	9.0	4.9	207
Any health insurance listed above [constructed]	87.0	74.1	76.7	83.8	3,584

Note: Questions were asked of all respondents, except as noted.

Web Table 8. Responses to overall financial well-being questions (by age)
Percent, except as noted

	Age					
	18–29	30–44	45–59	60+	Overall	N
Which one of the following best describes how well you are managing financially these days?						
Finding it difficult to get by	13.9	15.2	16.1	8.1	13.3	462
Just getting by	23.2	30.5	27.1	19.9	25.3	970
Doing okay	41.2	35.1	36.7	36.9	37.3	1,578
Living comfortably	19.9	17.9	19.2	34.5	23.0	1,088
Compared to five years ago (2008), would you say that you are better off, the same, or worse off financially?						
Much worse	9.5	13.7	16.0	9.7	12.4	469
Somewhat worse	19.2	19.2	22.7	26.5	22.0	945
About the same	28.8	31.9	33.3	41.6	34.2	1,462
Somewhat better off	23.6	22.9	18.7	15.7	20.0	849
Much better off	16.5	10.7	8.5	5.6	10.0	368

	Age					
	18 29	30–44	45–59	60+	Overall	N
During the next 12 months, do you expect your total income to be higher, about the same, or lower than during the past 12 months?						
Lower	15.8	13.1	17.6	17.8	16.1	689
About the same	50.1	55.2	63.7	70.9	60.5	2,559
Higher	29.3	28.6	16.8	10.1	20.7	802

Note: Questions were asked of all respondents, except as noted.

Web Table 9. Responses to housing questions (by age)
Percent, except as noted

	Age					
	18–29	30–44	45–59	60+	Over all	N
Please select all the reason below for why you rent your home rather than own your home? (asked of renters)						
It's cheaper to rent than own a home	17.2	18.2	35.0	24.9	22.8	232
It's more convenient to rent (for example, you can move easily)	26.5	26.0	19.6	24.3	24.4	259
I plan on moving in the near future	29.5	20.3	15.8	8.7	20.1	212
I can't qualify for a mortgage to buy a home	24.2	27.9	40.5	24.6	29.1	291
I can't afford the down payment to buy a home	48.6	48.0	45.9	33.2	45.3	444
I simply prefer to rent	14.4	14.0	23.5	34.0	19.6	207
I'm currently looking to buy a home	11.0	11.8	6.7	7.3	9.7	104
Other	7.9	5.1	10.5	15.5	8.9	112
Compared to five years ago (since 2008), do you think the value of your home today is higher, lower, or stayed the same? (asked of homeowners)						
Lower value	31.6	50.0	46.6	43.5	45.2	981
Value has stayed the same	22.0	15.1	20.1	20.7	19.5	479
Higher value	30.8	25.7	26.1	27.7	26.9	599
Don't Know	12.7	9.0	6.3	7.3	7.5	148
In the next 12 months, how much, if at all, do you think that home prices in your neighborhood will change? (asked of homeowners)						

Web Table 9. (Continued)

	Age					
	18–29	**30–44**	**45–59**	**60+**	**Over all**	**N**
Go down by more than 5 percent	1.2	3.2	4.5	3.1	3.4	92
Go down by 5 percent or less	5.6	6.4	5.4	3.1	4.9	122
Stay about the same	29.5	30.5	43.5	37.1	36.8	1,046
Go up by 5 percent or less	26.1	29.0	22.5	26.6	25.8	734
Go up by more than 5 percent	21.4	13.9	10.2	14.2	13.5	351
Don't know	15.0	16.9	13.5	15.5	15.1	377
Thinking about the past 12 months, did you want to sell your home, but did not or could not? (asked of homeowners)						
Yes, I put it on the market, but could not sell it	4.4	1.6	1.7	1.4	1.9	45
Yes, I wanted to sell, but did not put it on the market	9.1	11.6	9.4	7.1	9.1	232
No, I did not want to sell	79.2	80.9	86.6	89.6	85.6	2,378
No, I was able to sell my home, or it's currently on the market	4.5	4.2	1.7	1.4	2.5	61

Note: Questions were asked of all respondents, except as noted.

Web Table 10. Responses to credit behavior and availability questions (by age) Percent, except as noted

	Age					
	18–29	**30–44**	**45–59**	**60+**	**Overall**	**N**
In the past 12 months, have you put off applying for credit because you thought you might be turned down?						
No	77.4	74.7	76.8	88.7	79.5	3,394
Yes	20.2	22.9	22.0	10.0	18.7	676
If you were to apply for a mortgage today, how confident are you that your application would be approved?						
Confident	42.3	52.1	53.1	60.5	52.5	2,427
Not confident	32.2	33.4	31.3	20.0	29.0	1,056
Don't know	23.1	12.5	15.0	18.1	16.9	601

	Age					
	18–29	30–44	45–59	60+	Overall	N
If you were to apply for credit or a loan today (other than a mortgage), how confident are you that your application would be approved?						
Very confident	29.4	37.6	42.9	52.6	41.2	1,973
Somewhat confident	28.0	22.6	17.9	18.2	21.3	835
Not confident	23.0	26.6	26.1	13.5	22.3	787
Don't know	17.5	11.9	12.1	13.5	13.5	486
If you had to guess, how would you rate your current credit score (such as a FICO score)?						
Poor	11.1	14.5	15.8	5.0	11.6	397
Fair	11.9	15.9	12.3	7.0	11.7	419
Good	18.7	17.7	13.4	14.3	15.8	607
Very good	19.5	20.3	20.3	24.5	21.2	950
Excellent	14.5	21.4	26.0	36.0	25.0	1,271
Don't know my score or how to rate it	22.0	8.9	11.2	12.2	13.2	446
In the past 12 months, have you always paid your credit card bills in full each month? (asked of respondents with at least one credit card)						
No	40.6	51.7	48.3	32.1	43.0	1,366
Yes	58.6	48.2	50.9	67.8	56.6	1,886

Note: Questions were asked of all respondents, except as noted.

Web Table 11. Responses to savings behavior questions (by age) Percent, except as noted

	Age					
	18–29	30–44	45–59	60+	Overall	N
In 2012, would you say that your household's total spending was more than your income, that it was about the same as your income,or that you spent less than your income?						
Spending was less than income	36.0	36.1	36.3	42.0	37.7	1,622
Spending was same as income	39.3	37.3	39.7	37.4	38.4	1,589
Spending was more than income	20.0	24.7	22.1	19.6	21.7	850

Web Table 11. (Continued)

	Age					
	18–29	**30–44**	**45–59**	**60+**	**Overall**	**N**
If you were to lose your main source of income (e.g. job, government benefits), could you cover your expenses for 3 months by borrowing money, using savings, selling assets, or borrowing from friends/family? (asked of approximately one-half of respondents)						
No	42.5	49.9	45.0	31.8	42.2	805
Yes	53.9	48.0	53.4	66.6	55.6	1,291
Have you set aside emergency or rainy day funds that would cover your expenses for 3 months in case of sickness, job loss, economic downturn, or other emergencies? (asked of approximately one-half of respondents)						
No	63.0	63.6	64.1	41.7	57.9	1,055
Yes	33.2	32.6	34.3	56.3	39.4	899
Suppose that you have an emergency expense that costs $400. *Based on your current financial situation*, how would you pay for this expense? If you would use more than one method to cover this expense please select all that apply.						
Put it on my credit card and pay it off in full at the next statement	25.7	25.2	25.1	34.4	27.7	1,288
Put it on my credit card and pay it off over time	17.8	19.1	14.8	16.4	16.9	704
With the money currently in my checking/savings account or with cash	32.3	33.9	38.4	48.5	38.6	1,740
Using money from a bank loan or line of credit	4.3	2.3	3.0	3.3	3.2	138
By borrowing from a friend or family member	18.1	14.2	10.6	5.6	11.8	411
Using a payday loan, deposit advance, or overdraft	4.8	4.4	3.7	1.7	3.6	117
By selling something	11.0	12.5	8.2	6.7	9.5	351
I wouldn't be able to pay for the expense right now	18.1	20.0	23.8	13.2	18.9	628
Other	2.0	1.7	2.0	2.9	2.1	86

Note: Questions were asked of all respondents, except as noted.

Web Table 12. Responses to education and student loan questions (by age) Percent, except as noted

	Age					
	18–29	**30–44**	**45–59**	**60+**	**Overall**	**N**
Do you currently owe any money or have any loans that you used to pay for your own education?						
No	51.5	66.7	75.6	77.1	68.6	2,977
Yes	35.9	22.5	7.4	1.7	15.8	568
Does not apply	10.5	9.5	15.9	20.0	14.2	537
Do you currently owe any money or have any loans that you used to pay for your own education, your spouse's education, your child's education, or your grandchild's education? [constructed]						
No	57.5	66.7	81.6	93.3	75.8	3,177
Yes	42.5	33.3	18.4	6.7	24.2	957
Did you complete the most recent educational program for which you borrowed money? (asked of respondents with debt for their own education)						
No	19.8	27.4	30.4	36.2	24.3	139
Yes	41.5	54.7	50.2	59.2	47.9	281
Still enrolled in the program	38.1	17.9	19.4	4.6	27.5	146
Overall, how would you say the lifetime financial benefits of your most recent educational program compare to the lifetime *financial costs* to you of this education? (asked of respondents with debt for their own education)						
Much larger financial benefits than costs	23.2	22.8	27.6	27.9	23.7	128
Somewhat larger financial benefits than costs	20.1	16.9	16.6	12.9	18.3	106
About same financial benefits and costs	22.5	20.3	19.1	11.8	21.0	118
Somewhat smaller financial benefits than costs	11.3	14.6	8.3	0.0	11.8	69
Much smaller financial benefits than costs	22.8	24.8	28.4	47.4	24.9	143
Thinking about your current education and work experience, how confident are you that you have the skills necessary to get the kinds of jobs you want *now*? (asked of respondents who are not retired or disabled)						

Web Table 12. (Continued)

	Age					
	18–29	30–44	45–59	60+	Overall	N
Very confident	24.8	28.1	28.8	27.7	27.3	829
Somewhat confident	43.5	38.3	38.9	29.5	39.2	1126
Not confident	16.6	18.2	18.8	22.8	18.3	517
I am not currently in the workforce and I am not looking for a job	6.0	7.7	6.1	9.3	6.9	187
Don't know	5.7	6.1	6.6	10.3	6.5	162

Note: Questions were asked of all respondents, except as noted.

Web Table 13. Responses to retirement questions (by age)
Percent, except as noted

	Age					
	18–29	30–44	45–59	60+	Overall	N
How much thought have you given to the financial planning for your retirement? (asked of all respondents net yet retired)						
None at all	40.7	20.7	18.6	19.6	25.1	656
A little	27.3	26.1	20.1	19.0	23.8	705
Some	17.6	25.9	24.6	19.3	22.6	752
A fair amount	7.9	16.1	20.2	20.6	15.7	591
A lot	4.7	9.7	15.7	20.5	11.4	423
Which one of the following best describes your plan for retirement? (asked of all respondents net yet retired who have done some planning for retirement)						
I do not plan to retire	4.8	6.0	8.0	3.1	6.2	112
Work fewer hours as I get close to retirement	13.8	9.8	6.1	14.2	9.6	159
Retire from my current career, but then find a different full-time job	4.5	4.4	4.2	0.2	3.8	63

	Age					
	18–29	30–44	45–59	60+	Overall	N
Retire from my current career, but then find a different part-time job	14.8	13.2	18.1	16.6	15.8	304
Retire from my current career, but then work for myself	10.0	10.6	10.4	6.1	9.8	171
Work full time until I retire, then stop working altogether	34.6	29.2	22.1	14.6	25.4	434
Keep working as long as possible	15.8	21.6	21.1	28.1	21.3	373
Other	0.8	3.7	9.8	16.4	7.2	140
What type of retirement savings do you have? (asked of all respondents net yet retired)						
No retirement savings or pension	50.5	27.8	23.0	15.4	30.9	804
Social Security Old-Age benefits	17.5	31.5	46.4	67.6	36.3	1,318
401(k), 403(b), thrift or other defined contribution pension plan	30.3	52.8	47.8	37.1	43.7	1,508
Defined benefit pension through an employer	7.0	16.0	26.9	25.9	18.2	725
Individual Retirement Account (IRA)	11.2	23.5	29.2	31.9	23.0	874
Savings outside a retirement account (e.g., a brokerage account, savings account)	15.4	19.3	28.6	33.3	22.7	862
Real estate or land	4.4	8.9	16.1	20.5	11.3	463
Other	1.7	3.4	4.1	4.1	3.2	87
How are you planning to pay for your expenses in retirement? (asked of non-retired respondents who plan to retire and who have done some planning for retirement)						
Social Security Old-Age benefits	20.4	41.4	58.4	74.2	44.6	1,553
I will continue working	18.7	24.5	24.5	30.0	23.5	758

Web Table 13. (Continued)

	Age					
	18–29	**30–44**	**45–59**	**60+**	**Overall**	**N**
Spouse/partner will continue working	6.4	8.8	11.2	7.2	8.8	296
Defined benefit pension from work	7.3	16.1	26.8	29.0	18.5	708
401(k), 403(b), thrift or other defined contribution pension plan from work	31.6	46.0	43.5	30.2	39.7	1,321
Individual Retirement Account (IRA)	14.1	22.5	26.3	28.6	22.1	809
Savings outside a retirement account (e.g., a brokerage account, savings account)	19.3	23.3	24.9	29.2	23.4	832
Income from real estate or the sale of real estate	6.1	7.1	10.4	11.0	8.3	296
Income from a business or the sale of a business	4.6	3.7	3.1	4.5	3.8	137
Rely on children, grandchildren, or other family	4.6	1.9	2.6	1.7	2.8	79
I don't know	40.7	24.8	16.2	8.7	24.6	631
Other	1.1	2.4	4.8	5.5	3.1	94
What sources are you (and your spouse/partner) using to pay for your expenses in retirement? (asked of all respondents who are currently retired)						
Social Security Old-Age benefits		20.5	8.7	80.5	74.5	730
I have a job		40.2	9.1	5.2	5.8	64
My spouse/partner has a job		7.7	17.9	11.4	11.9	120
Defined benefit pension from work		20.5	48.8	44.2	44.3	470
401(k), 403(b), thrift or other defined contribution pension plan from work		4.4	12.5	19.1	18.5	210
Individual Retirement Account (IRA)		4.4	13.4	30.3	28.8	319

	Age					
	18–29	**30–44**	**45–59**	**60+**	**Overall**	**N**
Savings outside a retirement account (e.g., a brokerage account, savings account)		7.7	26.8	32.2	31.6	335
Income from real estate or the sale of real estate		0.0	9.8	8.8	8.8	90
Income from a business or the sale of a business		0.0	2.9	2.6	2.6	28
Relying on children, grandchildren, or other family		0.0	0.0	2.1	1.9	16
Other		0.0	4.9	6.0	5.9	48

Note: Questions were asked of all respondents, except as noted.

Web Table 14. Responses to health insurance and health-care expenses questions (by age)
Percent, except as noted

	Age					
	18–29	**30–44**	**45–59**	**60+**	**Overall**	**N**
During the past 12 months, was there a time when you needed any of the following, but didn't get it because you couldn't afford it?						
Prescription medicine (including taking less medication than prescribed)	15.4	17.8	17.4	9.1	14.9	532
To see a doctor	20.6	22.2	20.0	8.2	17.6	634
Mental health care or counseling	9.8	9.5	5.6	2.5	6.7	232
Dental care (including check-ups or routine cleaning)	25.1	30.6	27.7	19.5	25.7	972
To see a specialist (such as an OB/GYN, dermatologist, orthopedic surgeon, etc.)	12.0	17.2	10.8	5.9	11.4	427
Follow-up care (e.g., going to physical therapy sessions recommended by a doctor)	11.2	12.1	11.5	6.6	10.3	367

Web Table 14. (Continued)

	Age					
	18–29	**30–44**	**45–59**	**60+**	**Overall**	**N**
Any medical treatment listed above [constructed]	34.9	39.0	37.1	24.2	33.8	1,272
During the past 12 months, have you had any unexpected major medical expenses that you had to pay out of pocket (that were not completely paid for by insurance)?						
No	78.7	70.1	72.2	77.2	74.4	3,060
Yes	19.3	28.1	26.9	22.4	24.4	1,035
If you were to have a major unexpected medical expense that you had to pay for out of pocket, how likely is it that you that you would be able to pay your medical bills?						
Not likely	47.9	46.9	45.9	31.5	42.8	1,596
Somewhat likely	35.0	33.9	33.2	35.9	34.5	1,455
Very likely	15.3	17.6	19.9	31.7	21.4	1,041
Are you currently covered by any of the following types of health insurance or health coverage plans?						
Insurance through a current or former employer or union (of yourself or a family member)	52.8	58.8	58.0	40.6	52.5	2,336
Insurance purchased directly from an insurance company (by yourself or a family member)	12.5	8.4	7.8	23.9	13.2	580
Medicare, for people 65 or older, or people with certain disabilities	2.3	3.6	10.4	66.7	21.7	1,041
Medicaid, Medical Assistance, or any kind of government-assistance plan for those with low incomes or disability	11.3	12.4	14.0	12.1	12.5	406
TRICARE or other military health care	4.7	2.3	2.2	5.2	3.5	161
VA (including those who have ever used or enrolled for VA health care)	2.6	1.9	3.6	10.9	4.9	223
Indian Health Service	2.2	1.1	0.6	0.7	1.1	31

	Age					
	18–29	30–44	45–59	60+	Overall	N
Any other type of health insurance or health coverage plan	5.5	2.4	3.3	8.3	4.9	207
Any health insurance listed above [constructed]	75.8	79.4	83.9	94.5	83.8	3,584

Note: Questions were asked of all respondents, except as noted.

Web Table 15. Responses to overall financial questions (by gender) Percent, except as noted

	Gender			
	Male	Female	Overall	N
Which one of the following best describes how well you are managing financially these days?				
Finding it difficult to get by	11.7	14.8	13.3	462
Just getting by	24.0	26.5	25.3	970
Doing okay	39.9	34.8	37.3	1,578
Living comfortably	23.1	22.9	23.0	1,088
Compared to five years ago (2008), would you say that you are better off, the same, or worse off financially?				
Much worse	11.8	13.0	12.4	469
Somewhat worse	21.2	22.8	22.0	945
About the same	33.5	34.8	34.2	1,462
Somewhat better off	21.6	18.6	20.0	849
Much better off	10.1	9.8	10.0	368
During the next 12 months, do you expect your total income to be higher, about the same, or lower than during the past 12 months?				
Lower	15.3	16.9	16.1	689
About the same	58.0	62.9	60.5	2,559
Higher	23.8	17.8	20.7	802

Note: Questions were asked of all respondents, except as noted.

Web Table 16. Responses to housing questions (by gender)
Percent, except as noted

	Gender			
	Male	**Female**	**Overall**	**N**
Please select all the reason below for why you rent your home rather than own your home? (asked of renters)				
It's cheaper to rent than own a home	25.4	20.7	22.8	232
It's more convenient to rent (for example, you can move easily)	25.7	23.3	24.4	259
I plan on moving in the near future	20.8	19.6	20.1	212
I can't qualify for a mortgage to buy a home	29.7	28.7	29.1	291
I can't afford the down payment to buy a home	45.0	45.6	45.3	444
I simply prefer to rent	20.1	19.2	19.6	207
I'm currently looking to buy a home	8.8	10.4	9.7	104
Other	6.8	10.6	8.9	112
Compared to five years ago (since 2008), do you think the value of your home today is higher, lower, or stayed the same? (asked of homeowners)				
Lower value	46.1	44.4	45.2	981
Value has stayed the same	20.1	19.0	19.5	479
Higher value	27.4	26.5	26.9	599
Don't Know	5.5	9.5	7.5	148
In the next 12 months, how much, if at all, do you think that home prices in your neighborhood will change? (asked of homeowners)				
Go down by more than 5 percent	2.8	4.0	3.4	92
Go down by 5 percent or less	4.8	4.9	4.9	122
Stay about the same	35.0	38.7	36.8	1,046
Go up by 5 percent or less	29.4	22.3	25.8	734
Go up by more than 5 percent	15.7	11.4	13.5	351
Don't know	11.7	18.6	15.1	377
Thinking about the past 12 months, did you want to sell your home, but did not or could not? (asked of homeowners)				
Yes, I put it on the market, but could not sell it	2.2	1.6	1.9	45
Yes, I wanted to sell, but did not put it on the market	9.1	9.1	9.1	232
No, I did not want to sell	85.0	86.1	85.6	2,378
No, I was able to sell my home, or it's currently on the market	2.4	2.5	2.5	61

Note: Questions were asked of all respondents, except as noted.

Web Table 17. Responses to credit behavior and availability questions (by gender)
Percent, except as noted

	Gender			
	Male	**Female**	**Overall**	**N**
In the past 12 months, have you put off applying for credit because you thought you might be turned down?				
No	80.4	78.7	79.5	3,394
Yes	17.3	20.0	18.7	676
If you were to apply for a mortgage today, how confident are you that your application would be approved?				
Confident	55.4	49.8	52.5	2,427
Not confident	26.9	31.0	29.0	1,056
Don't know	15.6	18.1	16.9	601
If you were to apply for credit or a loan today (other than a mortgage), how confident are you that your application would be approved?				
Very confident	43.6	39.0	41.2	1,973
Somewhat confident	21.9	20.7	21.3	835
Not confident	20.4	24.0	22.3	787
Don't know	12.0	15.0	13.5	486
If you had to guess, how would you rate your current credit score (such as a FICO score)?				
Poor	9.7	13.4	11.6	397
Fair	11.6	11.8	11.7	419
Good	15.8	15.9	15.8	607
Very good	21.7	20.8	21.2	950
Excellent	27.3	22.9	25.0	1,271
Don't know my score or how to rate it	12.1	14.1	13.2	446
In the past 12 months, have you always paid your credit card bills in full each month? (asked of respondents with at least one credit card)				
No	41.1	44.8	43.0	1,366
Yes	58.2	55.0	56.6	1,886

Note: Questions were asked of all respondents, except as noted.

Web Table 18. Responses to savings behavior questions (by gender)
Percent, except as noted

	Gender			
	Male	Female	Overall	N
In 2012, would you say that your household's total spending was more than your income, that or that you spent less than your income?				
Spending was less than income	38.2	37.2	37.7	1,622
Spending was same as income	38.7	38.2	38.4	1,589
Spending was more than income	20.1	23.2	21.7	850
If you were to lose your main source of income (e.g. job, government benefits), could you cover your expenses for 3 months by borrowing money, using savings, selling assets, or borrowing from friends/family? (asked of approximately one-half of respondents)				
No	40.0	44.2	42.2	805
Yes	57.2	54.1	55.6	1,291
Have you set aside emergency or rainy day funds that would cover your expenses for 3 months in case of sickness, job loss, economic downturn, or other emergencies? (asked of approximately one-half of respondents)				
No	54.4	61.3	57.9	1,055
Yes	42.8	36.1	39.4	899
Suppose that you have an emergency expense that costs $400. *Based on your current financial situation*, how would you pay for this expense? If you would use more than one method to cover this expense please select all that apply.				
Put it on my credit card and pay it off in full at the next statement	29.5	26.0	27.7	1,288
Put it on my credit card and pay it off over time	16.9	17.0	16.9	704
With the money currently in my checking/savings account or with cash	39.4	37.9	38.6	1,740
Using money from a bank loan or line of credit	3.8	2.6	3.2	138
By borrowing from a friend or family member	11.1	12.4	11.8	411
Using a payday loan, deposit advance, or overdraft	3.4	3.8	3.6	117
By selling something	9.7	9.3	9.5	351
I wouldn't be able to pay for the expense right now	16.5	21.0	18.9	628
Other	1.8	2.5	2.1	86

Note: Questions were asked of all respondents, except as noted.

Web Table 19. Responses to education and student loan questions (by gender)
Percent, except as noted

	Gender			
	Male	**Female**	**Overall**	**N**
Do you currently owe any money or have any loans that you used to pay for your own education?				
No	72.0	65.5	68.6	2,977
Yes	14.8	16.7	15.8	568
Does not apply	11.6	16.6	14.2	537
Do you currently owe any money or have any loans that you used to pay for your own education, your spouse's education, your child's education, or your grandchild's education? [constructed]				
No	75.6	75.9	75.8	3,177
Yes	24.4	24.1	24.2	957
Did you complete the most recent educational program for which you borrowed money? (asked of respondents with debt for their own education)				
No	26.7	22.4	24.3	139
Yes	48.3	47.6	47.9	281
Still enrolled in the program	25.0	29.5	27.5	146
Overall, how would you say the lifetime *financial benefits* of your most recent educational program compare to the lifetime *financial costs* to you of this education? (asked of respondents with debt for their own education)				
Much larger financial benefits than costs	25.8	22.1	23.7	128
Somewhat larger financial benefits than costs	22.4	14.8	18.3	106
About same financial benefits and costs	17.0	24.3	21.0	118
Somewhat smaller financial benefits than costs	15.0	9.1	11.8	69
Much smaller financial benefits than costs	19.9	29.1	24.9	143
Thinking about your current education and work experience, how confident are you that you have the skills necessary to get the kinds of jobs you want *now*? (asked of respondents who are not retired or disabled)				
Very confident	31.0	23.8	27.3	829
Somewhat confident	40.6	37.8	39.2	1,126
Not confident	16.8	19.8	18.3	517
I am not currently in the workforce and I am not looking for a job	3.1	10.5	6.9	187
Don't know	6.3	6.7	6.5	162

Note: Questions were asked of all respondents, except as noted.

Web Table 20. Responses to retirement questions (by gender)
Percent, except as noted

	Gender			
	Male	Female	Overall	N
How much thought have you given to the financial planning for your retirement? (asked of all respondents net yet retired)				
None at all	22.6	27.6	25.1	656
A little	24.7	22.9	23.8	705
Some	22.4	22.8	22.6	752
A fair amount	16.1	15.3	15.7	591
A lot	12.6	10.3	11.4	423
Which one of the following best describes your plan for retirement? (asked of all respondents net yet retired who have done some planning for retirement)				
I do not plan to retire	6.0	6.5	6.2	112
Work fewer hours as I get close to retirement	8.6	10.5	9.6	159
Retire from my current career, but then find a different full-time job	4.8	2.8	3.8	63
Retire from my current career, but then find a different part-time job	17.8	13.8	15.8	304
Retire from my current career, but then work for myself	11.2	8.5	9.8	171
Work full time until I retire, then stop working altogether	27.2	23.7	25.4	434
Keep working as long as possible	17.8	24.9	21.3	373
Other	6.3	8.1	7.2	140
What type of retirement savings do you have? (asked of all respondents net yet retired)				
No retirement savings or pension	29.1	32.6	30.9	804
Social Security Old-Age benefits	38.3	34.5	36.3	1,318
401(k), 403(b), thrift or other defined contribution pension plan	45.2	42.2	43.7	1,508
Defined benefit pension through an employer	19.7	16.8	18.2	725
Individual Retirement Account (IRA)	23.7	22.3	23.0	874
Savings outside a retirement account (e.g., a brokerage account, savings account)	24.9	20.6	22.7	862

	Gender			
	Male	Female	Overall	N
Real estate or land	13.0	9.6	11.3	463
Other	3.1	3.4	3.2	87
How are you planning to pay for your expenses in retirement? (asked of non-retired respondents who plan to retire and who have done some planning for retirement)				
Social Security Old-Age benefits	46.3	43.0	44.6	1,553
I will continue working	25.6	21.6	23.5	758
Spouse/partner will continue working	8.2	9.3	8.8	296
Defined benefit pension from work	20.8	16.3	18.5	708
401(k), 403(b), thrift or other defined contribution pension plan from work	43.3	36.3	39.7	1,321
Individual Retirement Account (IRA)	22.8	21.4	22.1	809
Savings outside a retirement account (e.g., a brokerage account, savings account)	25.9	21.0	23.4	832
Income from real estate or the sale of real estate	10.0	6.7	8.3	296
Income from a business or the sale of a business	4.4	3.4	3.8	137
Rely on children, grandchildren, or other family	2.4	3.2	2.8	79
I don't know	21.3	27.8	24.6	631
Other	2.8	3.4	3.1	94
What sources are you (and your spouse/partner) using to pay for your expenses in retirement? (asked of all respondents who are currently retired)				
Social Security Old-Age benefits	74.1	74.8	74.5	730
I have a job	6.0	5.6	5.8	64
My spouse/partner has a job	14.9	9.3	11.9	120
Defined benefit pension from work	46.7	42.3	44.3	470
401(k), 403(b), thrift or other defined contribution pension plan from work	20.9	16.4	18.5	210
Individual Retirement Account (IRA)	31.5	26.4	28.8	319
Savings outside a retirement account (e.g., a brokerage account, savings account)	32.5	30.8	31.6	335
Income from real estate or the sale of real estate	9.6	8.2	8.8	90

Web Table 20. (Continued)

	Gender			
	Male	Female	Overall	N
Income from a business or the sale of a business	3.3	1.9	2.6	28
Relying on children, grandchildren, or other family	1.5	2.3	1.9	16
Other	5.9	5.9	5.9	48

Note: Questions were asked of all respondents, except as noted.

Web Table 21. Responses to health insurance and health-care expenses questions (by gender) Percent, except as noted

	Gender			
	Male	Female	Overall	N
During the past 12 months, was there a time when you needed any of the following, but didn't				
Prescription medicine (including taking less medication than prescribed)	11.9	17.7	14.9	532
To see a doctor	14.8	20.2	17.6	634
Mental health care or counseling	5.4	7.9	6.7	232
Dental care (including check-ups or routine cleaning)	22.4	28.9	25.7	972
To see a specialist (such as an OB/GYN, dermatologist, orthopedic surgeon, etc.)	7.6	14.9	11.4	427
Follow-up care (e.g., going to physical therapy sessions recommended by a doctor)	8.2	12.3	10.3	367
Any medical treatment listed above [constructed]	29.0	38.2	33.8	1,272
During the past 12 months, have you had any unexpected major medical expenses that you had to pay out of pocket (that were not completely paid for by insurance)?				
No	75.7	73.2	74.4	3,060
Yes	22.6	26.1	24.4	1,035
If you were to have a major unexpected medical expense that you had to pay for out of pocket, how likely is it that you that you would be able to pay your medical bills?				
Not likely	39.5	45.9	42.8	1,596

	Gender			
	Male	Female	Overall	N
Somewhat likely	35.7	33.3	34.5	1,455
Very likely	23.1	19.9	21.4	1,041
Are you currently covered by any of the following types of health insurance or health coverage plans?				
Insurance through a current or former employer or union (of yourself or a family member)	54.2	51.0	52.5	2,336
Insurance purchased directly from an insurance company (by yourself or a family member)	12.1	14.3	13.2	580
Medicare, for people 65 or older, or people with certain disabilities	20.1	23.1	21.7	1,041
Medicaid, Medical Assistance, or any kind of government-assistance plan for those with low incomes or disability	9.5	15.4	12.5	406
TRICARE or other military health care	4.4	2.8	3.5	161
VA (including those who have ever used or enrolled for VA health care)	7.7	2.3	4.9	223
Indian Health Service	1.3	0.9	1.1	31
Any other type of health insurance or health coverage plan	4.0	5.6	4.9	207
Any health insurance listed above [constructed]	82.8	84.7	83.8	3,584

Note: Questions were asked of all respondents, except as noted.

Web Table 22. Responses to overall financial well-being questions (by income) Percent, except as noted

	Income						
	Less than $25,000	$25,000–$49,999	$50,000–$74,999	$75,000–$99,999	$100,000 and greater	Overall	N
Which one of the following best describes how well you are managing financially these days?							
Finding it difficult to get by	25.7	13.3	8.8	3.5	2.1	13.6	452

Web Table 22. (Continued)

	Income						
	Less than $25,000	$25,000–$49,999	$50,000–$74,999	$75,000–$99,999	$100,000 and greater	Overall	N
Just getting by	34.7	31.3	22.9	16.2	10.4	25.7	944
Doing okay	29.8	38.0	42.1	49.5	37.7	37.2	1,508
Living comfortably	9.2	16.9	26.1	30.8	49.2	23.0	1,043
Compared to five years ago (2008), would you say that you are better off, the same, or worse off financially?							
Much worse	21.1	12.7	8.5	6.9	4.4	12.7	455
Somewhat worse	24.3	24.2	25.7	19.2	14.7	22.3	916
About the same	33.6	34.8	32.1	32.9	36.1	33.9	1,389
Somewhat better off	14.2	16.9	22.0	25.8	31.1	20.3	824
Much better off	6.0	9.9	11.6	15.2	13.8	10.2	359
During the next 12 months, do you expect your total income to be higher, about the same, or lower than during the past 12 months?							
Lower	18.8	15.3	12.7	13.5	18.3	16.3	668
About the same	63.8	60.7	64.8	60.9	55.7	61.6	2,477
Higher	15.8	23.4	21.9	24.7	25.4	21.1	784

Note: Questions were asked of all respondents, except as noted.

Web Table 23. Responses to housing questions (by income)
Percent, except as noted

	Income						
	Less than $25,000	$25,000–$49,999	$50,000–$74,999	$75,000–$99,999	$100,000 and greater	Overall	N
Please select all the reason below for why you rent your home rather than own your home? (asked of renters)							
It's cheaper to rent than own a home	24.7	22.0	24.2	8.7	24.9	23.1	229

	Income						
	Less than $25,000	**$25,000–$49,999**	**$50,000–$74,999**	**$75,000–$99,999**	**$100,000 and greater**	**Overall**	**N**
It's more convenient to rent (for example, you can move easily)	19.0	27.3	29.9	27.4	34.9	24.2	248
I plan on moving in the near future	14.5	22.6	27.3	35.4	22.9	20.0	205
I can't qualify for a mortgage to buy a home	35.5	30.3	23.8	18.4	10.2	29.8	290
I can't afford the down payment to buy a home	49.4	45.4	50.0	46.4	22.9	46.3	441
I simply prefer to rent	21.0	19.4	17.3	5.8	25.6	19.6	203
I'm currently looking to buy a home	6.7	12.1	13.2	14.6	11.7	9.7	101
Other	8.4	8.8	7.2	15.9	9.8	8.9	108
Compared to five years ago (since 2008), do you think the value of your home today is higher, lower, or stayed the same? (asked of homeowners)							
Lower value	46.0	45.3	46.5	45.2	44.5	45.5	946
Value has stayed the same	14.8	22.1	22.5	15.6	22.0	19.5	463
Higher value	24.4	26.2	26.5	32.0	27.9	27.0	576
Don't Know	14.3	6.1	4.0	6.6	4.8	7.4	140
In the next 12 months, how much, if at all, do you think that home prices in your neighborhood will change? (asked of homeowners)							
Go down by more than 5 percent	6.4	4.1	2.3	1.8	1.8	3.4	87
Go down by 5 percent or less	10.0	3.8	3.5	4.4	2.6	4.9	117
Stay about the same	32.0	41.8	41.4	37.9	33.2	37.0	1,010
Go up by 5 percent or less	13.9	23.6	26.8	33.7	36.2	26.6	722
Go up by more than 5 percent	11.2	10.1	14.2	11.9	19.7	13.7	341
Don't know	26.1	16.5	11.6	10.3	6.5	14.3	347
Thinking about the past 12 months, did you want to sell your home, but did not or could not? (asked of homeowners)							

Web Table 23. (Continued)

	Income						
	Less than $25,000	$25,000–$49,999	$50,000–$74,999	$75,000–$99,999	$100,000 and greater	Overall	N
Yes, I put it on the market, but could not sell it	3.5	1.9	0.4	1.2	1.8	1.8	43
Yes, I wanted to sell, but did not put it on the market	10.6	12.2	9.2	6.0	7.6	9.3	227
No, I did not want to sell	82.7	83.9	87.8	90.3	86.9	86.1	2,291
No, I was able to sell my home, or it's currently on the market	2.0	1.8	2.5	2.5	3.3	2.4	58

Note: Questions were asked of all respondents, except as noted.

Web Table 24. Responses to credit behavior and availability questions (by income)
Percent, except as noted

	Income						
	Less than $25,000	$25,000–$49,999	$50,000–$74,999	$75,000–$99,999	$100,000 and greater	Overall	N
In the past 12 months, have you put off applying for credit because you thought you might be turned down?							
No	70.2	77.6	84.2	87.4	90.8	79.6	3,251
Yes	28.7	20.8	15.3	11.5	8.3	19.3	668
If you were to apply for a mortgage today, how confident are you that your application would be approved?							
Confident	26.7	49.7	66.4	76.6	79.8	53.2	2,344
Not confident	42.9	35.4	23.9	15.8	12.7	29.8	1,037
Don't know	29.3	14.1	9.7	6.5	6.5	16.2	551

	Income						
	Less than $25,000	$25,000–$49,999	$50,000–$74,999	$75,000–$99,999	$100,000 and greater	Overall	N
If you were to apply for credit or a loan today (other than a mortgage), how confident are you that your application would be approved?							
Very confident	17.8	36.5	53.3	58.3	71.1	41.5	1,895
Somewhat confident	20.1	26.5	22.1	24.9	15.7	21.6	813
Not confident	36.6	25.5	16.1	11.3	8.1	23.0	776
Don't know	23.9	11.0	8.2	4.7	4.1	12.9	444
If you had to guess, how would you rate your current credit score (such as a FICO score)?							
Poor	20.3	14.1	7.2	4.0	3.6	12.0	391
Fair	16.0	13.6	10.0	10.2	5.0	11.9	410
Good	15.2	19.7	17.9	18.2	10.8	16.2	597
Very good	11.7	22.3	29.0	25.7	27.9	21.3	907
Excellent	10.6	20.4	30.3	35.1	48.9	25.3	1,229
Don't know my score or how to rate it	25.5	9.3	5.2	5.7	3.7	12.5	406
In the past 12 months, have you always paid your credit card bills in full each month? (asked of respondents with at least one credit card)							
No	48.7	49.0	42.4	41.4	34.1	43.4	1,337
Yes	51.2	51.0	57.5	58.6	65.9	56.5	1,808

Note: Questions were asked of all respondents, except as noted.

Web Table 25. Responses to savings behavior questions (by income)
Percent, except as noted

	Income						
	Less than $25,000	$25,000–$49,999	$50,000–$74,999	$75,000–$99,999	$100,000 and greater	Overall	N
In 2012, would you say that your household's total spending was more than your income, that it or that you spent less than your income?							
Spending was less than income	27.8	28.6	42.9	45.0	59.6	37.9	1,559

	Income						
	Less than $25,000	$25,000–$49,999	$50,000–$74,999	$75,000–$99,999	$100,000 and greater	Overall	N
Spending was same as income	41.5	43.3	38.1	38.4	29.3	38.9	1,537
Spending was more than income	29.6	27.1	18.6	16.0	10.5	22.4	834
If you were to lose your main source of income (e.g. job, government benefits), could you cover your expenses for 3 months by borrowing money, using savings, selling assets, or borrowing from friends/family? (asked of approximately one-half of respondents)							
No	66.8	46.6	30.3	29.6	15.4	43.1	792
Yes	31.6	52.3	69.7	70.1	83.9	55.9	1,253
Have you set aside emergency or rainy day funds that would cover your expenses for 3 months in case of sickness, job loss, economic downturn, or other emergencies? (asked of approximately one-half of respondents)							
No	77.8	64.2	51.0	50.7	32.2	59.5	1,024
Yes	21.4	34.0	47.4	49.3	67.5	39.5	858
Suppose that you have an emergency expense that costs $400. *Based on your current financial situation*, how would you pay for this expense? If you would use more than one method to cover this expense please select all that apply.							
Put it on my credit card and pay it off in full at the next statement	13.1	21.5	34.2	36.9	51.7	27.8	1,236
Put it on my credit card and pay it off over time	14.6	22.5	19.3	21.6	12.2	17.5	693
With the money currently in my checking/savings account or with cash	25.3	40.8	48.8	45.5	51.1	39.3	1,694
Using money from a bank loan or line of credit	1.9	5.0	5.1	4.3	1.4	3.3	136
By borrowing from a friend or family member	18.7	15.3	8.7	6.7	1.8	12.0	398

	Income						
	Less than $25,000	$25,000–$49,999	$50,000–$74,999	$75,000–$99,999	$100,000 and greater	Overall	N
Using a payday loan, deposit advance, or overdraft	6.0	4.8	2.3	1.7	0.4	3.7	116
By selling something	15.8	11.2	6.1	5.0	2.9	9.7	345
I wouldn't be able to pay for the expense right now	38.2	17.9	10.3	6.5	3.0	19.4	616
Other	3.1	2.5	1.8	1.5	1.1	2.2	85

Note: Questions were asked of all respondents, except as noted.

Web Table 26. Responses to education and student loan questions (by income)
Percent, except as noted

	Income						
	Less than $25,000	$25,000–$49,999	$50,000–$74,999	$75,000–$99,999	$100,000 and greater	Overall	N
Do you currently owe any money or have any loans that you used to pay for your own education?							
No	60.0	72.6	69.9	73.6	80.9	69.5	2,886
Yes	16.5	14.6	18.5	18.6	13.2	16.1	553
Does not apply	22.5	12.2	10.1	7.4	5.4	13.6	489
Do you currently owe any money or have any loans that you used to pay for your own education, your spouse's education, your child's education, or your grandchild's education? [constructed]							
No	80.3	76.6	73.1	65.0	72.6	75.2	3,028
Yes	19.7	23.4	26.9	35.0	27.4	24.8	931
Did you complete the most recent educational program for which you borrowed money? (asked of respondents with debt for their own education)							

Web Table 26. (Continued)

	Income						
	Less than $25,000	$25,000–$49,999	$50,000–$74,999	$75,000–$99,999	$100,000 and greater	Overall	N
No	32.5	24.8	23.3	16.3	13.9	24.5	135
Yes	41.5	40.4	53.0	52.9	65.3	48.4	277
Still enrolled in the program	26.0	34.8	23.7	28.5	20.9	26.9	140
Overall, how would you say the lifetime financial benefits of your most recent educational program compare to the lifetime financial costs to you of this education? (asked of respondents with debt for their own education)							
Much larger financial benefits than costs	20.2	23.4	26.1	26.5	28.4	23.9	126
Somewhat larger financial benefits than costs	16.1	13.4	21.0	30.2	15.9	18.3	104
About same financial benefits and costs	21.2	26.4	16.8	9.7	23.4	20.2	112
Somewhat smaller financial benefits than costs	11.5	10.1	11.1	13.5	14.9	11.9	68
Much smaller financial benefits than costs	31.0	26.4	24.2	20.2	17.5	25.5	141
Thinking about your current education and work experience, how confident are you that you have the skills necessary to get the kinds of jobs you want *now*? (asked of respondents who are not retired or disabled)							
Very confident	22.1	22.2	27.0	29.5	40.1	27.6	804
Somewhat confident	33.2	44.2	40.6	45.1	40.1	39.8	1,090
Not confident	23.3	23.1	18.0	14.5	11.8	18.9	506
I am not currently in the workforce and I am not looking for a job	7.0	5.8	10.2	5.3	6.0	6.9	182
Don't know	13.7	4.4	3.4	4.3	1.4	6.2	145

Note: Questions were asked of all respondents, except as noted.

Web Table 27. Responses to retirement questions (by Income)
Percent, except as noted

	Income						
	Less than $25,000	**$25,000–$49,999**	**$50,000–$74,999**	**$75,000–$99,999**	**$100,000 and greater**	**Overall**	**N**
How much thought have you given to the financial planning for your retirement? (asked of all respondents net yet retired)							
None at all	43.5	23.9	15.0	13.9	9.0	25.2	630
A little	20.9	24.7	31.9	27.0	19.6	24.0	682
Some	18.4	26.9	21.6	28.3	24.0	22.8	733
A fair amount	9.0	14.3	19.3	18.7	24.9	15.8	571
A lot	7.4	8.9	11.7	12.1	22.2	11.6	409
Which one of the following best describes your plan for retirement? (asked of all respondents net yet retired who have done some planning for retirement)							
I do not plan to retire	10.3	6.9	5.1	3.7	3.9	6.2	107
Work fewer hours as I get close to retirement	8.0	10.1	13.3	10.5	7.8	9.6	154
Retire from my current career, but then find a different full-time job	6.1	2.4	2.7	3.0	4.4	3.9	62
Retire from my current career, but then find a different part-time job	8.1	17.8	14.8	21.0	19.5	15.9	297
Retire from my current career, but then work for myself	9.3	8.2	9.0	11.5	12.3	10.1	167
Work full time until I retire, then stop working altogether	14.6	19.5	30.7	30.3	35.3	25.7	424
Keep working as long as possible	28.0	27.7	18.1	15.6	12.6	20.7	356
Other	14.1	7.2	5.8	3.6	3.8	7.2	137
What type of retirement savings do you have? (asked of all respondents net yet retired)							
No retirement savings or pension	54.1	32.1	18.2	12.9	9.8	31.0	776
Social Security Old-Age benefits	23.9	30.8	43.3	43.0	58.0	36.8	1,279

Web Table 27. (Continued)

	Income						
	Less than $25,000	$25,000–$49,999	$50,000–$74,999	$75,000–$99,999	$100,000 and greater	Overall	N
401(k), 403(b), thrift or other defined contribution pension plan	16.9	36.6	60.3	70.1	73.8	44.4	1,468
Defined benefit pension through an employer	6.8	13.6	22.0	29.0	36.6	18.6	712
Individual Retirement Account (IRA)	7.2	17.4	30.5	30.7	47.5	23.1	843
Savings outside a retirement account (e.g., a brokerage account, savings account)	7.5	17.9	26.3	35.0	47.9	23.1	841
Real estate or land	4.5	8.1	10.0	16.4	26.5	11.4	453
Other	4.3	3.2	2.4	3.1	3.1	3.4	87
How are you planning to pay for your expenses in retirement? (asked of non-retired respondents who plan to retire and who have done some planning for retirement)							
Social Security Old-Age benefits	32.1	45.2	56.0	46.7	59.8	45.5	1,516
I will continue working	19.0	30.9	24.2	27.2	23.2	24.1	742
Spouse/partner will continue working	4.6	9.2	12.8	11.5	11.9	9.0	292
Defined benefit pension from work	6.4	12.3	22.8	28.5	38.5	18.6	690
401(k), 403(b), thrift or other defined contribution pension plan from work	14.0	34.3	53.2	66.6	68.6	40.5	1,286
Individual Retirement Account (IRA)	8.1	16.8	27.7	31.0	44.8	22.4	785
Savings outside a retirement account (e.g., a brokerage account, savings account)	8.8	21.6	25.6	31.3	47.1	23.7	810
Income from real estate or the sale of real estate	3.7	7.9	5.5	10.3	19.6	8.5	290

	Income						
	Less than $25,000	$25,000–$49,999	$50,000–$74,999	$75,000–$99,999	$100,000 and greater	Overall	N
Income from a business or the sale of a business	2.4	2.6	5.3	6.4	5.9	4.0	136
Rely on children, grandchildren, or other family	2.9	3.3	3.9	2.1	2.3	3.0	79
I don't know	40.9	22.1	16.9	14.6	9.1	24.2	597
Other	3.6	3.7	2.6	2.1	3.1	3.2	92
What sources are you (and your spouse/partner) using to pay for your expenses in retirement? (asked of all respondents who are currently retired)							
Social Security Old-Age benefits	77.5	75.2	78.3	75.0	71.3	76.0	702
I have a job	5.1	6.3	5.9	4.8	8.1	5.9	61
My spouse/partner has a job	5.9	8.4	13.4	13.9	29.5	11.9	112
Defined benefit pension from work	23.5	47.0	57.4	55.9	65.8	45.1	453
401(k), 403(b), thrift or other defined contribution pension plan from work	10.2	16.4	25.7	26.8	30.1	19.2	207
Individual Retirement Account (IRA)	17.5	27.9	37.1	43.1	41.0	30.0	312
Savings outside a retirement account (e.g., a brokerage account, savings account)	21.1	33.8	37.4	41.2	41.3	32.4	323
Income from real estate or the sale of real estate	5.4	11.2	10.4	11.2	10.8	9.2	88
Income from a business or the sale of a business	1.8	2.0	1.7	4.2	4.2	2.5	26
Relying on children, grandchildren, or other family	2.2	2.8	0.4	4.4	0.0	2.0	16
Other	5.9	5.8	7.3	8.7	3.7	6.2	48

Note: Questions were asked of all respondents, except as noted.

Web Table 28. Responses to health insurance and health-care expenses questions (by income)
Percent, except as noted

	Income						
	Less than $25,000	**$25,000–$49,999**	**$50,000–$74,999**	**$75,000–$99,999**	**$100,000 and greater**	**Overall**	**N**
During the past 12 months, was there a time when you needed any of the following, but didn't get because you couldn't afford it?							
Prescription medicine (including taking less medication than prescribed)	24.9	17.6	11.5	7.0	3.8	15.4	527
To see a doctor	26.2	23.4	15.2	9.0	4.7	18.1	624
Mental health care or counseling	12.5	6.1	4.5	4.3	1.4	6.9	228
Dental care (including check-ups or routine cleaning)	38.3	32.8	23.1	14.0	7.3	26.5	955
To see a specialist (such as an OB/GYN, dermatologist, orthopedic surgeon, etc.)	16.3	15.2	9.7	7.7	3.4	11.8	420
Follow-up care (e.g., going to physical therapy sessions recommended by a doctor)	16.5	12.5	7.4	8.2	2.2	10.7	362
Any medical treatment listed above [constructed]	47.8	43.1	30.4	20.7	11.5	34.6	1,247
During the past 12 months, have you had any unexpected major medical expenses that you had to pay out of pocket (that were not completely paid for by insurance)?							
No	72.7	75.1	74.4	72.0	78.0	74.3	2,927
Yes	26.6	24.6	25.6	27.2	21.8	25.2	1,018
If you were to have a major unexpected medical expense that you had to pay for out of pocket, how likely is it that you that you would be able to pay your medical bills?							

	Income						
	Less than $25,000	**$25,000–$49,999**	**$50,000–$74,999**	**$75,000–$99,999**	**$100,000 and greater**	**Overall**	**N**
Not likely	63.4	51.0	36.2	18.5	16.8	43.1	1,540
Somewhat likely	26.7	34.5	39.3	47.7	38.3	34.9	1,402
Very likely	9.1	14.1	24.4	33.0	44.9	21.6	1,002
Are you currently covered by any of the following types of health insurance or health coverage plans?							
Insurance through a current or former employer or union (of yourself or a family member)	25.0	48.5	67.0	75.8	83.3	52.9	2,247
Insurance purchased directly from an insurance company (by yourself or a family member)	12.5	15.5	14.7	14.4	8.9	13.1	551
Medicare, for people 65 or older, or people with certain disabilities	28.2	22.6	19.9	18.4	12.4	21.8	998
Medicaid, Medical Assistance, or any kind of government-assistance plan for those with low incomes or disability	30.0	8.3	3.3	1.3	2.1	12.7	394
TRICARE or other military health care	2.3	3.9	4.7	4.4	4.5	3.7	159
VA (including those who have ever used or enrolled for VA health care)	6.4	5.9	4.0	5.3	2.4	5.1	220
Indian Health Service	2.4	0.4	1.3	0.1	0.0	1.1	30
Any other type of health insurance or health coverage plan	7.4	5.5	2.5	3.3	3.1	5.0	203
Any health insurance listed above [constructed]	74.4	81.0	90.1	95.6	96.3	84.6	3,453

Note: Questions were asked of all respondents, except as noted.

Web Table 29. Responses to overall financial well-being questions (by education)
Percent, except as noted

	Education					
	Less than high school	**High school**	**Some college**	**Bachelor's degree or higher**	**Overall**	**N**
Which one of the following best describes how well you are managing financially these days?						
Finding it difficult to get by	23.5	14.8	13.7	7.3	13.3	462
Just getting by	28.3	31.9	25.4	17.1	25.3	970
Doing okay	32.4	33.8	39.0	41.2	37.3	1,578
Living comfortably	12.9	18.4	21.0	33.8	23.0	1,088
Compared to five years ago (2008), would you say that you are better off, the same, or worse off financially?						
Much worse	17.2	14.1	12.1	9.1	12.4	469
Somewhat worse	25.5	24.2	22.3	18.1	22.0	945
About the same	34.1	36.5	30.2	35.6	34.2	1,462
Somewhat better off	11.8	15.7	23.7	24.2	20.0	849
Much better off	7.2	8.1	10.2	12.7	10.0	368
During the next 12 months, do you expect your total income to be higher, about the same, or lower than during the past 12 months?						
Lower	20.0	16.4	16.8	13.6	16.1	689
About the same	62.6	65.9	58.5	56.1	60.5	2,559
Higher	12.1	15.4	21.8	28.5	20.7	802

Note: Questions were asked of all respondents, except as noted.

Web Table 30. Responses to housing questions (by education)
Percent, except as noted

	Education					
	Less than high school	**High school**	**Some college**	**Bachelor's degree or higher**	**Overall**	**N**
Please select all the reason below for why you rent your home rather than own your home? (asked of renters)						
It's cheaper to rent than own a home	24.7	21.3	23.3	23.2	22.8	232

	Education					
	Less than high school	**High school**	**Some college**	**Bachelor's degree or higher**	**Overall**	**N**
It's more convenient to rent (for example, you can move easily)	16.5	20.5	26.8	32.2	24.4	259
I plan on moving in the near future	13.1	18.1	20.7	26.9	20.1	212
I can't qualify for a mortgage to buy a home	32.1	29.5	31.6	23.6	29.1	291
I can't afford the down payment to buy a home	48.1	43.1	43.9	48.2	45.3	444
I simply prefer to rent	23.1	21.0	17.2	18.3	19.6	207
I'm currently looking to buy a home	8.1	8.0	10.8	11.6	9.7	104
Other	2.9	9.8	9.5	10.7	8.9	112
Compared to five years ago (since 2008), do you think the value of your home today is higher, lower, or stayed the same? (asked of homeowners)						
Lower value	45.3	44.5	44.1	46.9	45.2	981
Value has stayed the same	11.4	19.9	21.0	20.0	19.5	479
Higher value	31.3	25.2	26.1	28.2	26.9	599
Don't Know	10.8	9.6	8.0	4.0	7.5	148
In the next 12 months, how much, if at all, do you think that home prices in your neighborhood will change? (asked of homeowners)						
Go down by more than 5 percent	5.7	3.0	4.4	2.4	3.4	92
Go down by 5 percent or less	11.6	4.9	5.0	3.2	4.9	122
Stay about the same	28.1	40.6	36.9	35.5	36.8	1,046
Go up by 5 percent or less	13.2	19.5	24.0	35.6	25.8	734
Go up by more than 5 percent	11.6	10.6	15.2	15.2	13.5	351
Don't know	28.4	20.9	14.1	7.9	15.1	377
Thinking about the past 12 months, did you want to sell your home, but did not or could not? (asked of homeowners)						
Yes, I put it on the market, but could not sell it	2.1	1.9	1.4	2.2	1.9	45
Yes, I wanted to sell, but did not put it on the market	7.3	10.8	9.6	7.7	9.1	232
No, I did not want to sell	82.6	84.3	86.2	86.8	85.6	2,378
No, I was able to sell my home, or it's currently on the market	4.7	1.6	1.8	3.2	2.5	61

Note: Questions were asked of all respondents, except as noted.

Web Table 31. Responses to credit behavior and availability questions (by education)
Percent, except as noted

	Education					
	Less than high school	**High school**	**Some college**	**Bachelor's degree or higher**	**Overall**	**N**
In the past 12 months, have you put off applying for credit because you thought you might be turned down?						
No	64.4	79.1	76.9	88.6	79.5	3,394
Yes	30.7	19.6	21.0	10.6	18.7	676
If you were to apply for a mortgage today, how confident are you that your application would be approved?						
Confident	30.0	44.7	50.8	71.4	52.5	2,427
Not confident	37.1	33.1	31.9	18.8	29.0	1,056
Don't know	29.1	20.9	15.5	9.1	16.9	601
If you were to apply for credit or a loan today (other than a mortgage), how confident are you that your application would be approved?						
Very confident	22.2	33.3	37.7	60.7	41.2	1,973
Somewhat confident	17.5	22.1	21.8	21.6	21.3	835
Not confident	32.0	26.0	25.3	11.5	22.3	787
Don't know	23.7	17.3	13.4	5.7	13.5	486
If you had to guess, how would you rate your current credit score (such as a FICO score)?						
Poor	19.5	14.3	13.2	4.1	11.6	397
Fair	12.4	13.3	13.1	8.5	11.7	419
Good	14.9	17.2	18.4	12.3	15.8	607
Very good	10.5	18.5	21.5	28.1	21.2	950
Excellent	11.1	18.4	21.5	41.0	25.0	1,271
Don't know my score or how to rate it	28.1	17.2	10.2	5.3	13.2	446
In the past 12 months, have you always paid your credit card bills in full each month? (asked of respondents with at least one credit card)						
No	48.6	46.3	48.1	35.3	43.0	1,366
Yes	50.8	53.1	51.4	64.5	56.6	1,886

Note: Questions were asked of all respondents, except as noted.

Web Table 32. Responses to savings behavior questions (by education)
Percent, except as noted

	Education					
	Less than high school	**High school**	**Some college**	**Bachelor's degree or higher**	**Overall**	**N**
In 2012, would you say that your household's total spending was more than your income, that it or that you spent less than your income?						
Spending was less than income	29.3	33.0	36.0	47.5	37.7	1,622
Spending was same as income	40.2	41.0	39.6	33.8	38.4	1,589
Spending was more than income	26.3	23.6	21.8	17.7	21.7	850
If you were to lose your main source of income (e.g. job, government benefits), could you cover your expenses for 3 months by borrowing money, using savings, selling assets, or borrowing from friends/family? (asked of approximately one-half of respondents)						
No	65.8	51.3	41.9	23.4	42.2	805
Yes	29.6	46.6	55.8	75.5	55.6	1,291
Have you set aside emergency or rainy day funds that would cover your expenses for 3 months in case of sickness, job loss, economic downturn, or other emergencies? (asked of approximately one-half of respondents)						
No	74.0	68.4	55.7	42.8	57.9	1,055
Yes	22.0	29.8	39.7	56.0	39.4	899
Suppose that you have an emergency expense that costs $400. *Based on your current financial situation*, how would you pay for this expense? If you would use more than one method to cover this expense please select all that apply.						
Put it on my credit card and pay it off in full at the next statement	8.6	18.9	23.5	48.6	27.7	1,288
Put it on my credit card and pay it off over time	17.0	17.3	18.8	14.7	16.9	704
With the money currently in my checking/savings account or with cash	23.6	35.1	41.3	45.5	38.6	1,740

Web Table 32. (Continued)

	Education					
	Less than high school	High school	Some college	Bachelor's degree or higher	Overall	N
Using money from a bank loan or line of credit	4.2	3.4	3.3	2.4	3.2	138
By borrowing from a friend or family member	16.4	14.4	12.4	6.5	11.8	411
Using a payday loan, deposit advance, or overdraft	7.3	4.1	4.3	1.0	3.6	117
By selling something	14.7	10.5	10.2	5.7	9.5	351
I wouldn't be able to pay for the expense right now	35.6	25.9	17.7	6.0	18.9	628
Other	2.5	2.8	2.3	1.2	2.1	86

Note: Questions were asked of all respondents, except as noted.

Web Table 33. Responses to education and student loan questions (by education)
Percent, except as noted

	Education					
	Less than high school	High school	Some college	Bachelor's degree or higher	Overall	N
Do you currently owe any money or have any loans that you used to pay for your own education?						
No	65.7	69.2	67.8	70.0	68.6	2,977
Yes	8.0	7.6	19.3	24.0	15.8	568
Does not apply	23.2	22.1	11.0	5.6	14.2	537
Do you currently owe any money or have any loans that you used to pay for your own education, your spouse's education, your child's education, or your grandchild's education? [constructed]						

	Education					
	Less than high school	**High school**	**Some college**	**Bachelor's degree or higher**	**Overall**	**N**
No	85.0	85.3	72.1	65.6	75.8	3,177
Yes	15.0	14.7	27.9	34.4	24.2	957
Did you complete the most recent educational program for which you borrowed money? (asked of respondents with debt for their own education)						
No	29.9	36.9	34.3	11.5	24.3	139
Yes	56.1	23.5	24.9	73.1	47.9	281
Still enrolled in the program	14.0	39.7	39.9	15.3	27.5	146
Overall, how would you say the lifetime financial benefits of your most recent educational program compare to the lifetime *financial costs* to you of this education? (asked of respondents with debt for their own education)						
Much larger financial benefits than costs	30.2	15.3	27.5	22.7	23.7	128
Somewhat larger financial benefits than costs	19.6	20.7	14.5	20.3	18.3	106
About same financial benefits and costs	13.2	19.5	23.1	20.8	21.0	118
Somewhat smaller financial benefits than costs	6.6	9.0	8.8	15.7	11.8	69
Much smaller financial benefits than costs	30.3	35.0	26.0	20.0	24.9	143
Thinking about your current education and work experience, how confident are you that you have the skills necessary to get the kinds of jobs you want *now*? (asked of respondents who are not retired or disabled)						
Very confident	21.5	20.7	25.0	36.8	27.3	829
Somewhat confident	30.1	39.1	42.2	39.4	39.2	1,126
Not confident	22.2	21.0	18.7	14.5	18.3	517
I am not currently in the workforce and I am not looking for a job	10.3	8.7	6.1	4.9	6.9	187
Don't know	12.2	9.3	5.6	3.3	6.5	162

Note: Questions were asked of all respondents, except as noted.

Web Table 34. Responses to retirement questions (by education)
Percent, except as noted

	Education					
	Less than high school	High school	Some college	Bachelor's degree or higher	Overall	N
How much thought have you given to the financial planning for your retirement? (asked of all respondents net yet retired)						
None at all	48.6	35.3	22.6	8.2	25.1	656
A little	21.0	22.8	25.4	24.2	23.8	705
Some	14.0	21.2	24.1	26.0	22.6	752
A fair amount	5.4	11.7	16.7	22.9	15.7	591
A lot	6.7	8.2	10.0	17.9	11.4	423
Which one of the following best describes your plan for retirement? (asked of all respondents net yet retired who have done some planning for retirement)						
I do not plan to retire	11.5	6.9	6.4	4.9	6.2	112
Work fewer hours as I get close to retirement	12.3	12.0	7.2	9.4	9.6	159
Retire from my current career, but then find a different full-time job	8.9	3.4	3.3	3.6	3.8	63
Retire from my current career, but then find a different part-time job	17.4	10.9	17.0	17.6	15.8	304
Retire from my current career, but then work for myself	11.7	5.8	9.2	12.5	9.8	171
Work full time until I retire, then stop working altogether	9.6	26.4	24.7	27.9	25.4	434
Keep working as long as possible	18.5	24.3	22.4	19.2	21.3	373
Other	7.1	10.1	8.7	4.5	7.2	140
What type of retirement savings do you have? (asked of all respondents net yet retired)						
No retirement savings or pension	52.8	38.2	31.1	14.7	30.9	804
Social Security Old-Age benefits	24.3	29.6	35.3	48.8	36.3	1,318

	Education					
	Less than high school	**High school**	**Some college**	**Bachelor's degree or higher**	**Overall**	**N**
401(k), 403(b), thrift or other defined contribution pension plan	20.7	31.5	42.0	66.4	43.7	1,508
Defined benefit pension through an employer	6.3	12.2	16.9	30.1	18.2	725
Individual Retirement Account (IRA)	5.5	14.1	19.0	42.5	23.0	874
Savings outside a retirement account (e.g., a brokerage account, savings account)	7.6	14.1	21.3	38.6	22.7	862
Real estate or land	3.5	7.1	11.6	18.1	11.3	463
Other	2.1	4.1	3.3	2.7	3.2	87
How are you planning to pay for your expenses in retirement? (asked of non-retired respondents who plan to retire and who have done some planning for retirement)						
Social Security Old-Age benefits	28.8	39.9	45.7	54.5	44.6	1,553
I will continue working	16.0	20.4	23.9	29.3	23.5	758
Spouse/partner will continue working	7.3	8.0	9.2	9.6	8.8	296
Defined benefit pension from work	8.3	12.4	17.5	29.6	18.5	708
401(k), 403(b), thrift or other defined contribution pension plan from work	17.6	26.7	39.7	61.6	39.7	1,321
Individual Retirement Account (IRA)	4.1	12.9	17.5	42.9	22.1	809
Savings outside a retirement account (e.g., a brokerage account, savings account)	6.0	14.5	21.4	41.1	23.4	832
Income from real estate or the sale of real estate	3.1	7.0	6.9	13.0	8.3	296
Income from a business or the sale of a business	3.8	2.6	3.9	5.0	3.8	137

Web Table 34. (Continued)

	Education					
	Less than high school	**High school**	**Some college**	**Bachelor's degree or higher**	**Overall**	**N**
Rely on children, grandchildren, or other family	2.9	2.7	2.6	3.1	2.8	79
I don't know	37.5	32.2	25.0	11.6	24.6	631
Other	3.7	3.2	3.3	2.7	3.1	94
What sources are you (and your spouse/partner) using to pay for your expenses in retirement? (asked of all respondents who are currently retired)						
Social Security Old-Age benefits	83.4	76.1	69.8	74.1	74.5	730
I have a job	3.5	4.5	6.1	8.1	5.8	64
My spouse/partner has a job	17.6	10.4	8.5	15.4	11.9	120
Defined benefit pension from work	25.1	41.6	44.4	55.3	44.3	470
401(k), 403(b), thrift or other defined contribution pension plan from work	4.3	20.0	17.1	23.7	18.5	210
Individual Retirement Account (IRA)	14.0	26.7	27.9	38.3	28.8	319
Savings outside a retirement account (e.g., a brokerage account, savings account)	16.9	25.4	33.0	43.8	31.6	335
Income from real estate or the sale of real estate	5.5	9.5	9.8	8.0	8.8	90
Income from a business or the sale of a business	0.9	1.0	2.2	5.7	2.6	28
Relying on children, grandchildren, or other family	7.2	1.9	1.8	0.0	1.9	16
Other	2.9	4.4	8.0	6.6	5.9	48

Note: Questions were asked of all respondents, except as noted.

Web Table 35. Responses to health insurance and health-care expenses questions (by education) Percent, except as noted

	Education					
	Less than high school	High school	Some college	Bachelor's degree or higher	Overall	N
During the past 12 months, was there a time when you needed any of the following, but didn't						
Prescription medicine (including taking less medication than prescribed)	24.7	16.2	15.0	9.6	14.9	532
To see a doctor	25.6	18.0	19.1	12.5	17.6	634
Mental health care or counseling	9.8	4.5	8.4	6.0	6.7	232
Dental care (including check-ups or routine cleaning)	33.6	27.3	29.8	17.0	25.7	972
To see a specialist (such as an OB/GYN, dermatologist, orthopedic surgeon, etc.)	15.9	11.0	12.3	9.3	11.4	427
Follow-up care (e.g., going to physical therapy sessions recommended by a doctor)	15.2	10.4	10.9	7.7	10.3	367
Any medical treatment listed above [constructed]	45.9	34.9	36.0	25.5	33.8	1,272
During the past 12 months, have you had any unexpected major medical expenses that you had to pay out of pocket (that were not completely paid for by insurance)?						
No	73.8	75.9	72.8	74.5	74.4	3,060
Yes	22.9	22.7	26.3	25.0	24.4	1,035
If you were to have a major unexpected medical expense that you had to pay for out of pocket, how likely is it that you that you would be able to pay your medical bills?						
Not likely	60.9	50.6	43.2	27.1	42.8	1,596
Somewhat likely	27.2	34.0	33.4	38.9	34.5	1,455

Web Table 35. (Continued)

	Education					
	Less than high school	**High school**	**Some college**	**Bachelor's degree or higher**	**Overall**	**N**
Very likely	9.2	14.1	21.8	33.5	21.4	1,041
Are you currently covered by any of the following types of health insurance or health coverage plans?						
Insurance through a current or former employer or union (of yourself or a family member)	27.0	44.0	51.4	72.7	52.5	2,336
Insurance purchased directly from an insurance company (by yourself or a family member)	14.2	13.9	13.0	12.2	13.2	580
Medicare, for people 65 or older, or people with certain disabilities	24.5	26.3	21.4	16.0	21.7	1,041
Medicaid, Medical Assistance, or any kind of government-assistance plan for those with low incomes or disability	30.5	16.7	11.0	2.6	12.5	406
TRICARE or other military health care	3.2	3.3	3.7	3.8	3.5	161
VA (including those who have ever used or enrolled for VA health care)	6.5	4.8	5.7	3.6	4.9	223
Indian Health Service	2.8	1.2	1.1	0.4	1.1	31
Any other type of health insurance or health coverage plan	6.4	6.4	4.4	3.2	4.9	207
Any health insurance listed above [constructed]	74.1	80.9	82.9	91.6	83.8	3,584

Note: Questions were asked of all respondents, except as noted.

INDEX

R

S

T

U

V

W

Y